VIOLENCE ON TELEVISION
What the viewers think

VIOLENCE ON TELEVISION
What the viewers think

Barrie Gunter

Head of Research
Independent Broadcasting Authority

Mallory Wober

Deputy Head of Research
Independent Broadcasting Authority

 John Libbey
LONDON · PARIS   IBA

British Library Cataloguing in Publication Data

Gunter, Barrie
    Violence on television: what the viewers think
    1. Great Britain. Television programmes. Violence
    I. Title   II. Wober, Mallory
    302.2'345

    ISBN 0-86196-171-4
    ISBN 0-86196-172-2 pbk

Published by
John Libbey & Company Ltd
80/84 Bondway, London SW8 1SF, England (01) 582 5266
John Libbey Eurotext Ltd
6 rue Blanche, 92120 Montrouge, France (1) 47 35 85 52

Typesetting in Century by E E Owens & Co Ltd, London SE15 4AZ
Printed in Great Britain by Whitstable Litho Ltd, Whitstable, Kent

Foreword

By John Whitney, Director-General of the IBA

At the Independent Broadcasting Authority, we believe that the opinions of viewers — the consumers of television — are a crucial part of the debate on television violence. And Parliament, through the Broadcasting Act, formally requires the IBA to be responsible for "ascertaining the state of public opinion" on the programmes that independent broadcasting provides.

Accordingly, IBA researchers have investigated in depth viewers' responses on a range of issues relating to violence in general and responses to particular programmes.

This IBA research is not, however, a "one-off" snapshot of what the viewers currently think about violence on television. It is part of a wide-ranging and continuous IBA research effort on many aspects of the relationship between television and our society. Every year since 1970, we have conducted a large survey — *Attitudes to Broadcasting* — which seeks viewers' opinions on (amongst other things) violence, offensiveness and programme standards generally. Dr Barrie Gunter, the IBA's Head of Research, is one of the country's acknowledged experts on the subject of violence and television. As he says in his summing up of his present report, his surveys show that public opinion about violence is varied rather than weighted all in one direction. Much depends on how the questions are put. Most of his sample felt that there are too many violent programmes on television, though they did not feel overwhelmingly that television violence had a harmful impact. Against the background of this properly cautious analysis, what this whole body of research shows is that while public interest in the subject of television violence fluctuates, viewers' attitudes have remained remarkably stable over time. A majority always claim that they have not seen anything they find offensive on television; the significant minority who are offended rate bad language higher than violence.

The research reported in *this* paper shows that most viewers are discriminating in their judgements about television violence. The majority of viewers imply by their attitudes that they want neither a laissez-faire nor a heavy-handed approach to the regulation of programme standards. They want an informative framework of regulation within which they can take responsibility for their own choices.

Violence on Television: What the viewers think is *not* about possible links between television and people's behaviour. It is not designed to probe the question of whether there is a relationship between television violence and violence (including crime) in real life. This question has been posed many times, but a direct causal link has never been convincingly established. We at the IBA are, however, concerned that the portrayal of violence on television *may*, over a period of time, have a desensitising or trivialising effect particularly on children. We are also very concerned about the small minority who say that violent programmes sometimes make them *feel* violent and about the possibility that in individual cases this may be one of the factors making them *act* violently. We have therefore commissioned two independent studies: one exploring patterns in television viewing and aggression in families, and one exploring the potentially desensitising effects of television on school children. This research is expected to be completed in Spring 1989.

The research effort of the IBA is directed towards informing the judgements on programme standards that the Authority is required by Parliament to make. But there are many other influences that are brought to bear on these judgements; not the least of them is public concern, however expressed, on issues that relate, whether directly or not, to what appears on the screen.

In the light of public concern following the Hungerford tragedy, the Members of the IBA have resolved that levels of violence on television should continue to be reduced, and that an even greater degree of vigilance over the portrayal of violence in ITV and Channel 4 programmes should be exercised.

Since Hungerford, the IBA has taken the following steps:

— more stringent procedures have been introduced for the previewing, certificating and editing of overseas and acquired material (ie which has not been made under the broad principles and good broadcasting practice contained in the IBA's Television Programme Guidelines and the IBA's Code on the Portrayal of Violence). All ITV-acquired mini-series are now being viewed by the ITV Film Clearance Committee and reported on to Programme Controllers;

— imported action/adventure programmes tend to contain more violent incidents. Previously, a maximum of five and a half hours per week of overseas material was allowed in peak time, between 6.30pm and 10.30pm; the IBA has now reduced this to *four hours* per week;

— the IBA has also strengthened its continuous monitoring of violence on ITV and Channel 4 programmes. The number of monitors on its panel has been increased. An enhanced monitoring system for recording the amount, content and nature of the portrayal of violence has been introduced. This will provide a more systematic method for measuring and classifying television violence. We will produce a comparative analysis of violent content over the twelve months from September 1987.

The debate about television violence continues, as indeed the debate on a matter of such importance to our society should. We have to be responsive to a wide range of opinions. Our research on *Violence on Television: What the viewers think* is, we believe, an important contribution to the debate.

John Whitney
Director General
January 1988

Contents

Summary

This monograph presents findings from almost 20 surveys of public opinion about violence on television. Its aim is to investigate what the viewers think about television violence. The surveys probe general opinions about television violence as well as perceptions of violence in particular types of programmes (e.g. drama, news) and in named television series. In some cases opinions about television violence were elicited without direct prompts while, in other instances, respondents were asked to indicate their agreement or disagreement with explicit statements of opinion about violence on television.

Opinions were found to vary quite a lot with the type of question being asked and with the type of television output being asked about. When asked explicitly about it, a majority of respondents indicated some concern about the amount of violence on television and about its possible harmful effects on viewers. Most respondents felt that there are too many violent programmes on television, though they did not feel overwhelmingly that television violence had a harmful impact.

However, alongside these opinions was a widespread feeling that parents should take greater care over what their children watch because young viewers were perceived to be naive in their discriminations between fact and fantasy and because they might therefore develop ill-conceived ideas about violence in consequence. All the same, our respondents revealed some awareness of the important role played by television in reflecting events that occur in real life. The press were perceived as often as not to exaggerate the effects of television violence on children, though this remained an important issue on which discussion should be continued. Many adult viewers harbour some concern about the potential harm television violence may have on young minds. Turning their attention to personal reactions to programmes, most viewers do not feel that they themselves are adversely affected by watching television violence. There was, however, a tiny, though worrying, minority who stated that sometimes they could feel quite violent after watching crime programmes. The meaning of this admission is not entirely clear and is being investigated further. However, this small component of the viewing population, no matter how tiny, must and does remain in the minds of broadcasters as a responsibility about which they are concerned and aware. Further opinions indicated that the public favour restrictions on when violent programmes are scheduled and wish to have more information and guidance about the content of programmes from the broadcasters, either in the form of warning symbols shown on screen or detail about programmes in television magazines and newspapers.

Despite concerns about the possible impact of television violence on younger viewers we found that parents extensively watch crime drama series with their children and few believe that these programmes have any harmful influences. When respondents' attention was focused on named television series produced either in the UK or USA, a variety of opinions emerged, not all of which were consonant with attitudes concerning a more generalised concept of 'violence on television'. These opinions provided an interesting and valuable contrast, however, since they were based on concrete examples of violent portrayals actually seen in specific programmes.

Despite fairly widespread agreement with statements that television contains too much violence, this opinion was much less commonplace in connection with particular television series. Sizeable proportions of respondents perceived the use of violence by fictional law enforcers mostly to be justified, although this opinion did vary across different series and was not always an opinion held by the majority. In general, fictional police were not seen as being more trigger happy than was necessary, but neither were they perceived by most respondents to behave like real police.

There were reservations about the suitability for children of both UK and US crime-drama productions. Exceptional cases were *Minder* and *The A-Team*. However, a further qualification is needed at this point. It emerged that respondents were really concerned about children watching these programmes unaccompanied by an adult. Most tended to feel that these programmes were suitable for family viewing. Indeed, nearly all the series on which opinions were obtained were televised outside of designated 'family viewing time'. *The A-Team* was the most prominent exception.

In the case of *The A-Team*, for the most part, highly favourable opinions emerged. Most respondents did not perceive the show to be excessively violent; most felt that it was unreal and humorous, and few judged it to be unsuitable for children or likely to frighten or disturb them.

In general, evaluations of UK and US crime drama series were positive and indicated that they are widely appreciated. And despite some respondents' reservations about the suitability of certain series for younger audiences, few said they would be pleased to see any of these series taken off the screen.

Several surveys are reported which investigated public opinion towards the coverage of violent events in the news. Topics covered included Northern Ireland, the Falklands conflict and civil disturbances in some of Britain's major cities. Respondents surveyed in England and Northern Ireland both agreed with the view that there was too much attention given to the province in television news broadcasts, although attitudes towards two documentary series about the troubles indicated that viewers felt they had had a positive effect. When asked at the time of the Falklands conflict, how much of the conflict and its consequences should be shown, around four out of ten respondents wanted to be shown British forces and Argentine forces in action, including pictures of the injured and dying. Rather more restraint was favoured, however, when it came to showing innocent sufferers, such as bereaved families.

Opinions about the coverage of civil disturbances in some of Britain's inner cities indicated that viewers believed that television news had enhanced certain areas of understanding but not others. Television news had shown the problems faced by the police when trying to control such incidents, but did not always provide adequate explanation of why they occurred in the first place.

In summing up, this collection of surveys reveals that public opinion about violence on television is varied rather than weighted all in one direction. Much depends on how questions about it are put, however, and whether or not they refer to general or specific areas of television output. Concerns about violence, whether shown in drama and entertainment programmes or in news programmes, do exist with respect to particular kinds of portrayals or reports among certain segments of the audience. On balance, however, the British viewing public does not express extremes of concern. Respondents surveyed in this body of research felt there was a need for some restraint on the part of the broadcasters and for special vigilance and care over programmes shown at times when many children are likely to be watching. Overall, public opinion seemed to indicate support for a system of regulation which is sensitive to existing values and tastes and which operates within a climate of shared responsibility among both broadcasters and viewers with regard to what is televised and what is defined as acceptable rather than strict censorship .

CHAPTER ONE

CONCERN IN PUBLIC ABOUT VIOLENCE ON TELEVISION

Introduction

From the earliest days of television there has been concern about the portrayal of violence in programmes. Over the years, more funding and research effort has been invested in the study of television violence than in any other aspect of television output. It is one of the most researched areas in the social sciences. Despite all this, there is still considerable disagreement among the experts about the existence of links between violence on the screen and the development of aggressive dispositions or incitement to violence of those who watch it.

A consensus of opinion among researchers may never be reached. Nevertheless, evidence has been published which points to possible harmful side-effects of viewing television violence. This has been accompanied by reports of widespread and growing public anxiety which has led to calls for stricter controls over the showing of violence in programmes.

Calls for the control of violence on television, however, necessitate some consideration of what is meant by violence in the first place. Ultimately, the implementation of controls over television violence is a practical problem. Somebody, somewhere has to decide what to cut out and what to leave in programmes. It is easy enough publicly to condemn violence on television, but far less easy to arrive at a system of guidelines and control through monitoring which takes full account of the values and tastes and possible vulnerability of the people who matter – namely the audience.

We may all have some idea in our heads of what we mean by violence, but

1

the truth of the matter is that what one person sees as violent may not be seen in the same way by someone else. Yet, for all that has been debated and written about television violence, there have been few serious attempts among either critics or researchers to provide meaningful and representative definitions of violence in terms of the tastes of the television audience, and to say precisely what it is on the screen that needs to be controlled.

All too often the opinions of the viewers themselves are forgotten or ignored. Broadcasters are often accused of allowing too much violence on to our television screens. Traditional methods for measuring how much violence there is on television, however, have not normally taken into account what viewers perceive to be violent. Typically, the violence of a programme is assessed in terms of the number of incidents it contains which fall within a framework of classification devised by the researchers themselves. There is not usually any attempt to find out if viewers would agree with the researchers in the way they have defined violence. Yet violence is a complex feature of programmes and in recent years research evidence has emerged which shows that viewers sensitivities to it may be highly discriminating (Gunter, 1985). Until this fact is taken on board by all those who investigate or criticise television violence, we cannot hope to achieve a balanced and representative judgement about whether or not television today is excessively violent, or a proper understanding of its impact upon the audience.

In this monograph we are concerned with viewers' opinions about television violence. These opinions can be broken down into two broad categories. First, we examine general ideas about violence on television without special reference to particular areas of output. Secondly, we look at attitudes towards violence in specific types of programmes or in named television series.

At this point, it is important to make a distinction between three different questions which reflect frequently voiced concerns about television violence about which discussion is often very muddled. Furthermore, the interpretations placed on the different sorts of research that are needed to provide appropriate answers to these questions often tend to be misconceived. This indicates a poor understanding of the limitations of different research procedures and what they are capable of demonstrating.

The voluminous writings about television violence can conveniently be broken down into discussions about just three major questions. First, is there too much violence on TV? To answer this question, we need to consider what we mean by violence in the first place, and then how best to assess the presence of violence in programmes. Criticisms of TV violence are often targetted at specific programmes. Typically though, the criteria of how violent a particular programme happens to be derive from simple and questionable incident counts. We need to know as well what viewers think about programmes, whether they recognise them as violent, or not.

Secondly, does TV violence cause social violence? Many newspaper stories tend to assume uncritically that this link has been firmly established. Such stories make good newspaper copy, but seldom look at all the facts carefully enough to provide an accurate, irrefutable case that it is televised violence that has been independently responsible for instigating individual imitative acts of violence, let alone being able to sustain a general case, that portrayals of one kind of violence may prompt aggression of a different kind. There is only equivocal evidence that television in a broad sense is a significant factor contributing to levels of crime and violence in society. There have been isolated cases, however, where individuals have performed aggressive or dangerous stunts producing harmful or tragic results either for someone else or them-selves, where their actions have borne some resemblance to portrayals shown in films at the cinema or in television broadcasts which they may have seen. These incidents are fortunately rare though unfortunately are also unpredictable and therefore can be difficult to control or prevent.

Thirdly, what do people think about TV violence? How concerned are viewers about violence on TV? We often hear that public concern about TV violence is widespread and that anxieties are growing. Typically, however, such statements are unsubstantiated by any systematic evi-dence. This last issue is the one we focus on in this monograph. We present evidence from a series of nationwide opinion polls which asked viewers in general what they thought about violence on TV and viewers of particular programmes what they felt about the violence contained in the episodes they had watched. Although we found that opinions varied depending on the types of questions and types of viewers, our findings suggest that the matter is more complex than the popular press and some lobby groups and politicians would have us believe. We believe that the strengths of our research lie in the fact that it derives from large representative samples of viewers in this country and that they are given the opportunity to present detailed opinions about television programmes they have actually watched.

Finally, we have to be and are aware of the problem that it is possible for a threshold of acceptance to be lowered so that, for example, with increased familiarity with a phenomenon some initial opposition to it becomes dissipated. Thus, it is argued that public behaviour has become more frank, so that bad language that was felt to be taboo two decades ago has now become tolerated. Similarly, discussion or advertisement of topics such as sanitary protection, haemorrhoids and contraceptive devices is considered more acceptable now than hitherto. Thus, there are two kinds of content submitted to a "test" of public acceptability and it is not to be taken for granted that acceptability is the test of whether the material is beneficial or not. Improved personal hygiene is almost incontestably beneficial, and increased acceptability for discourse about this can be taken as recognition of this benefit.

The same seal of approval may be a valid test of utility for screen entertainment which depicts violence; or it may be mistaken. This is not what is being examined in this report. What can be examined, though it calls for skill in interpretation of the evidence, is whether thresholds of acceptance may have become lowered as an initial effect of a phenomenon that may be deleterious in this and other ways. If such thresholds can be interpreted as still operating in the same way as they did a decade or more ago, then standards of expressed offence can at least be taken as helpfully comparable across time.

CHAPTER TWO

SOURCES OF PUBLIC CONCERN AND OFFENCE

We begin by examining, in a fairly general sense, public feelings and opinion about TV violence. Is violence a widespread source of offence to viewers? And is there a growing public awareness of distasteful violence in programmes? Some of those actively engaged in the public debate about these issues have indicated that there is widespread public concern about violence on television. Several surveys conducted by the IBA have revealed little in the way of widespread concern at least on the scale inferred by many newspaper reports. As we will also see, however, levels of 'concern' can vary depending on the types of question one asks. In this monograph we will consider two general types of attitudes: first, general public attitudes towards violence on television; secondly, attitudes towards specific programmes – including some programmes which have been singled out by some anti-TV violence lobbyists for particular criticism. Both of these will be examined in some detail in following chapters. For the moment though we will present evidence on the extent to which violence emerged unprompted among viewers as a source of perceived offence or falling standards on television.

Violence as a source of offence

At the beginning of November 1985 the *Daily Telegraph* published results from a national Gallup Poll which showed that 60 percent of people agreed with the statement "There is too much violence in TV entertainment shows". In a further Gallup Poll, results published by the same newspaper in September, 1987, revealed that 56 percent of a national survey sample agreed that "there is too much violence on television".

While this at first seems very damning evidence and, taken by itself corresponds to a result in one of the IBA's own surveys, the problem with this kind of approach is that it focuses viewers' attention acutely on violence alone and does not get to grips with the significance of violence for them in the broader context of all other aspects of TV which influence reasons for watching and reactions to what is seen.

If we take away the prompt and leave people to name their own problem areas on TV, we find that violence is mentioned much less often. For instance, in its annual survey of *Attitudes to Broadcasting*, the IBA asks people if they have seen anything on TV in the past year that they found offensive. Among those who say they have, further probing reveals sources of offence.

Firstly we can take a look at trends in perceived offence since 1970. On average around 40 percent of respondents claimed to have seen something on television in the past year that offended them (see Figure 2.1). Perceived offensive material on ITV and BBC run closely in parallel throughout this 15-year period with ITV staying fairly consistently a percentage point or two above BBC1. From one year to the next, the difference is usually quite small, however. From 1980 up to 1985 there

Figure 2.1 Trends in perceived offence 1970-1987

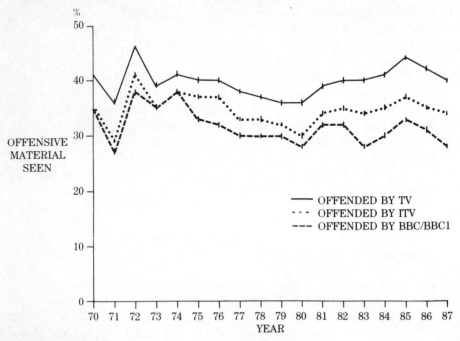

SOURCE: IBA ATTITUDES TO ADVERTISING
NOTE: PERCENTAGES ARE OF ALL ADULTS WITH A TV SET

was a slight, though steady upward trend in percentages of viewers who said they had seen something that had offended them on television. Since then, however, the figures for both channels have indicated a decline in perceived offence.

We need to know what are the sources of offence. Further probing reveals just what these are. A subsequent question in the IBA's annual public opinion survey asks about the nature of the material which is found offensive. People are free to answer in their own words, and their responses are classified afterwards. The three most often named sources of offence are bad language, violence and sex. In 1986, bad language remained the prime complaint for all four TV channels (mentioned on average per channel by 15 percent of all viewers), with violence coming second (11 percent average across channels) and sex following in third place (10 percent). Recent trends for ITV indicate an increase in the extent to which both bad language and violence are mentioned by those who have been offended at all. Looking at longer-term trends, however, it can also be seen that there is no greater tendency for violence to be named as a cause of offence on TV today than ten years ago (see Figure 2.2). The recent picture indicates that there was an increase in concern over the five years up to 1985 compensating for a fall in the previous five.

Figure 2.2 Type of offence as a percentage of those offended at all by ITV

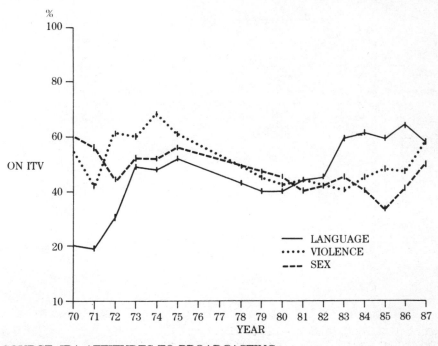

SOURCE: IBA ATTITUDES TO BROADCASTING

There was a slight fall in 1986, followed once again by an apparent rise in concern in 1987. The latter upward trend, however, may in part reflect the high profile television violence has received as an issue of public discussion during 1987.

This increase may be taken as one sign that a general desensitisation has not occurred. If a threshold of acceptability as a consequence of regular viewing had fallen, then fewer people would have replied that they were offended – and this is not what has been found. The result does not go as far as dismissing a possible case that desensitisation may have occurred in one particular field, for example, that of violence. But if that was the case, one would have to argue that sensitivity in other areas had increased to a marked extent, to produce an "average" overall rise in reported offence. Such a field-specific phenomenon, with sensitivity increasing sharply in one area to outbalance insensitivity or tolerance on another realm is psychologically inconsistent and unlikely. The indication, therefore, is that subsequent opinion judgments we shall discuss can be considered as usefully comparable, based on some reasonably stable standard across the years.

The figures for BBC show similar trends to those for ITV (see Figure 2.3). Both these sets of figures to some extent exaggerate the level of

Figure 2.3 Type of offence as a percentage of those offended at all by BBC/BBC1

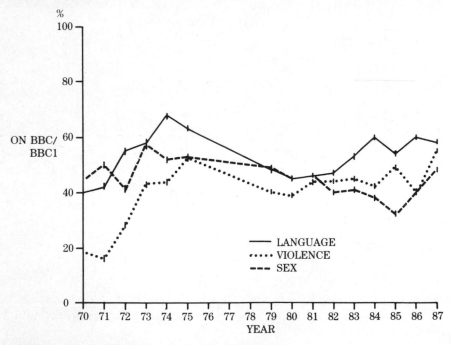

SOURCE: IBA ATTITUDES TO ADVERTISING

concern about TV violence, however. Between 40 and 50 percent say they have been offended by violent content on TV, but these are percentages of those who were offended at all – and not percentages of all viewers, i.e. including those who said they had not seen anything offensive on TV. In the national surveys conducted over the five years from 1983 to 1987, just over four out of ten respondents (43%) on average claimed to have seen or heard anything offensive on TV at all over the previous year.

If we put levels of offence caused by TV violence into that sort of perspective, then we can see that fewer than one in five viewers spontaneously mention violence as a source of recent offence to them on television. This level of responding is no different from that recorded ten years ago (see Figure 2.4), although ten years ago it had increased from the levels observed five years previously.

These results still do not justify complacency on the part of the broadcasters in continuing to be vigilant in their monitoring of programme output and implementation of programme guidelines and codes of

Figure 2.4 Those offended by violence as percentage of population 1970-1985

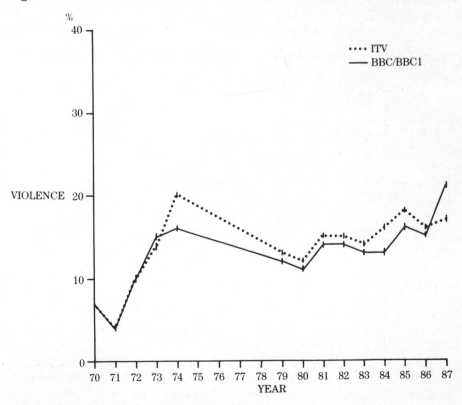

SOURCE: IBA ATTITUDES TO ADVERTISING

practice. Even one in five viewers represents a sizeable number of people. However, such findings do offer a more balanced appraisal of the extent to which violence is a prominent concern which, unprompted, springs to the minds of viewers as a source of major concern.

Those offended by bad language number slightly more than those offended by violence (see Figure 2.5 compared with 2.4), while those

Figure 2.5 Those offended by bad language as percentage of population 1970-1987

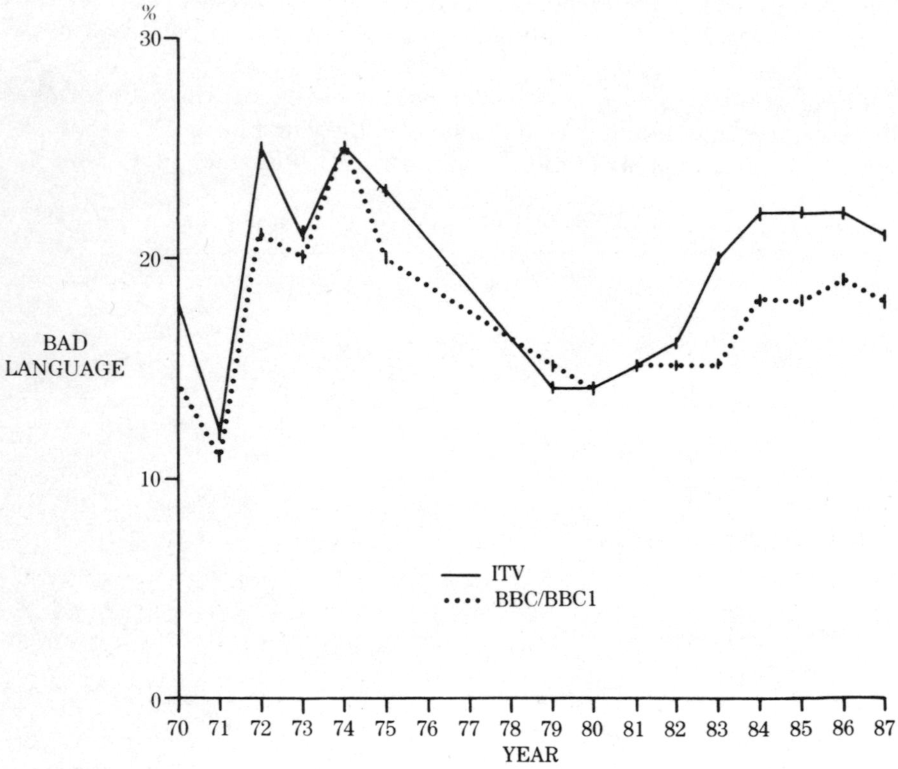

SOURCE: IBA ATTITUDES TO ADVERTISING

offended by sexual content number slightly less (see Figure 2.6). Recent years have, however, witnessed an upward trend in concern about bad language, while concern about sex declined during the early 1980s, before showing a slight upward trend during the last year.

Figure 2.6 Those offended by sex as percentage of population 1970-1987

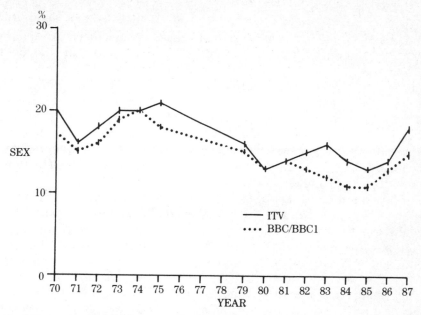

SOURCE: IBA ATTITUDES TO ADVERTISING

Violence and the Standards of Television

Trends spanning the past fifteen years or more reveal that the frequency with which viewers have perceived offensive material on television has fluctuated to some extent. By and large, year-on-year comparisons indicate considerable stability of public opinion. And certainly looking over the last ten years, there is very little difference between the extent of perceived offence registered in 1976 and 1986.

The extent to which various causes of offence were reported by viewers has fluctuated since 1970 when the IBA's annual public opinion survey began. In 1970 on ITV sexual content was of primary concern, followed fairly closely by violence, with bad language some distance behind in third place. Since the early 1980s, however, profanity has become a more prominent concern. After reaching a peak of concern in the mid-1970s, however, violence and sex have attracted steadily fewer and fewer mentions ever since. Although the trend for violence reversed during the mid-1980s, the proportions of respondents saying they were offended by violence on ITV and BBC1 in 1986 decreased marginally from the 1985 levels, while no change was seen for BBC2, and a one percentage point increase occurred for Channel 4.

11

Finally, it is worth mentioning that this chapter has focussed on the issue of what viewers say they find offensive on TV when prompted to do so. In the broader context of what viewers have to say about the standards of TV and in particular, about causes of a decline in the quality of output, mentions of "too much violence", "too much sex" or "too much bad language" feature even less prominently.

In the IBA *Attitudes to Broadcasting* survey for 1986 (IBA, 1987), over five out of ten television viewers (51%) said they thought programme standards on television in general had stayed the same over the past year. Around one in ten (11%) thought that standards had improved, while one in three (34%) thought they had got worse, a fall of five percent on the 1985 figure. Opinions about television in general were reinforced by those given for individual television channels.

Further questioning about sources of dissatisfaction among those respondents who said that they believed TV standards had fallen, revealed that the reason mentioned most often without prompting was, as in all previous years, that there were too many repeats. This was mentioned by 20 percent of all respondents with regard to ITV, 22 percent for BBC1, 11 percent for BBC2 and 10 percent for Channel Four.

The results for 1986 showed that the numbers saying there is too much violence on TV, in the context of falling standards, decreased, especially for ITV (from 8% to 5% of all viewers), on 1985 levels. Smaller decreases emerged with regard to opinions about the other channels too. There were also decreases in the numbers saying there was "too much sex" or "too much bad language".

Perhaps the major conclusions to emerge from these findings are first, that the extent of public concern about violence on TV can depend considerably on the way it is investigated and measured. Different types of questions give rise to different levels of concern. Secondly, whether in the broad context of the perceived standards of TV or within the narrower frame of reference of perceived offence on screen, the extent to which viewers spontaneously mention violence either as a reason for declining standards on TV or of offensiveness on TV does not indicate widespread public concern. As we focus in still further on the concept of violence, and on the different forms or contexts in which it can occur on TV, is there any evidence that viewers are concerned at least about certain types of violence? We turn to examine this question in the next chapter.

CHAPTER THREE

GENERAL OPINIONS ABOUT VIOLENCE ON TELEVISION

Only a minority of viewers mention violence in the context of sources of offence on TV and just a tiny minority do so when thinking about reasons for the falling standards of programmes. What happens to levels of public concern and to the nature of public opinion about TV violence when the attention of survey respondents is focused on that subject? Do opinions become sharper and anxiety more pronounced? Or do viewers exhibit a variety of opinions which depend on the kinds of violence they are asked about? Some viewers may hold broad concerns about the depiction of any violence, while other, more discriminating individuals may exhibit more focussed reservations which apply to some portrayals in certain contexts, but not to others. In this chapter, we want to narrow down the discussion to some extent, to ask more tellingly about the acceptance of violence on TV.

The findings we introduce next derive from questions placed with the TOP (Television Opinion Panel), a national omnibus survey run for its clients by the Broadcasters' Audience Research Board (BARB). These questions were answered by panel members who were also required to fill in viewing diaries to indicate their appreciation ratings of the programmes they saw during the survey week.

Is TV violence thought to be harmful or harmless?

The first group of items we can take a look at concern viewers' opinions about whether TV violence has harmful effects, or is harmless, or indeed whether it has beneficial influences. Results presented in Table 3.1 show that six items dealt with potential harms, five with a harmless role of violence, and one with possible beneficial effects. Across our national viewing panel, there was much more widespread agreement with items endorsing potential harms than with those that endorsed the potential harmlessness of TV violence.

Nearly eight out of ten respondents felt that people are justified in being concerned about the impact of TV violence on children today. At the same time, more than six out of ten believed that children will imitate violence seen on television, that TV violence frightens children and that children can become desensitised to violence through seeing it portrayed on television. Slightly smaller percentages of respondents believed that television violence can make children aggressive and that it is bad for

Table 3.1 Television violence as harmful, harmless or beneficial

	Agree	Neither	Disagree
	%	%	%
Harmful effects of TV violence			
People are justified in being concerned about the impact of TV violence on children today	78	17	5
Children will imitate the violence they see on TV	64	22	14
Watching TV programmes containing violence often frightens children unnecessarily	63	20	17
If children often watch TV programmes containing violence, they get accustomed to violence	61	25	14
By watching TV programmes containing violence, children become aggressive	58	27	15
Watching programmes containing violence is bad for children's sleep	57	27	16
Average	64	22	14
Harmlessness of TV violence			
It can do no harm if children watch programmes containing violence once in a while	33	34	33
It can do no harm if children sometimes get a bit frightened from TV violence	23	22	55
Children forget violent programmes very quickly	19	32	49
Watching violence on TV has hardly any influence on children at all	11	15	74
Average	19	23	58
Beneficial effects of TV violence			
When children watch TV programmes containing violence, they get rid of some of their own aggression	9	33	58

SOURCE: IBA/BARB

children's sleep. In summary, when given direct prompts, many viewers believe that TV violence may have potentially harmful effects on children, influencing their behaviour and disturbing them emotionally.

On four out of five items which identified TV violence as being, on balance, harmless, those who disagreed far outnumbered those who agreed with such sentiments. There were mixed feelings about whether seeing TV violence once in a while can do children any real harm. The same proportion of respondents agreed and disagreed with this belief. However, respondents did not believe on the whole that it can do no harm for children to be frightened by TV violence, or that violence has no effect on children or that they quickly forget about violent programmes. Between a half and three quarters rejected the latter beliefs. Very few respondents indeed thought that children could discharge their own aggression through watching violence on TV. There was very little public support for the notion of catharsis.

How important is parental control of children's viewing?

While there is some public concern with the notion of showing violence on TV, to what extent do viewers think that children could be afforded some protection or guidance by their parents? How seriously do people believe that parents should take their responsibilities in this respect? The general feeling that emerged here was that viewers do feel that parents have a responsibility to control what their children watch. As we can see

Table 3.2 Importance of parental control over children's viewing

	Agree	Neither	Disagree
	%	%	%
Control over children's viewing			
Parents should take greater care over the TV programmes their children watch at home	88	9	3
Too few parents these days are prepared to control what their children watch on TV	80	12	8
Children's contact with TV programmes containing violence should be put off for as long as possible	68	20	12
If parents explain the programmes to them, there is no objection to children watching TV programmes with violence	23	21	56
I don't mind if children want to amuse themselves with programmes containing violence	9	20	71

SOURCE: IBA/BARB

from the opinions shown in Table 3.2 nearly nine out of ten respondents felt that parents should take greater care over the TV their children watch. And a further eight out of ten believed that parents these days seldom take the trouble to control their children's viewing. A majority of around two out of three respondents felt that children's contact with televised violence should be put off for as long as possible. Few claimed that they did not mind about children amusing themselves with violent programmes if they wanted to, and even if parents take the trouble to explain programmes to youngsters, few respondents were in favour of children watching programmes with violence.

Perceptions of children's impressions of violence

We examined two issues here. Firstly, was there a general belief that children are capable of making certain basic distinctions between fantasy and reality on television? This distinction is very important and is known to mediate viewers' response to TV violence. Secondly, what sort of picture of the world are children likely to develop from watching television violence? Is TV violence thought to be likely to produce a distorted view of the world as a cosy and safe place? Some results are shown in Table 3.3.

More adult respondents rejected than accepted the proposition that children are discriminating. More than one in five thought that children understand that TV violence is not real compared with just over half who believed they did not. Opinions were somewhat less well-formed on the issue of whether children quickly learn to distinguish fantasy from reality

Table 3.3 Beliefs about children's perceptions of TV violence

	Agree %	Neither %	Disagree %
Discriminating perceptions of TV violence			
I believe that children learn very quickly to distinguish between the violence shown on fictional and reality programmes	28	35	37
Children understand well enough that TV violence is not real	21	29	50
Impressions of violence			
TV programmes containing violence give children the impression that murder is a day-to-day affair	60	24	16
If TV programmes contain no violence, children get too rosy a picture of the outside world	35	30	35

SOURCE: IBA/BARB

programming. More respondents felt that children did not make this distinction than who felt that they do, while a substantial minority were undecided.

Most respondents believed that TV programmes containing violence give children the impression of a violent world. Fewer felt that by taking violence out of programmes, children would get too rosy a picture of the world – although as many were likely to agree with this view as to disagree.

The violence issue in perspective

The TV violence issue regularly hits the headlines. We have already seen that the public believe the issue to be an important one. In particular, people are concerned about potential harms televised violence may do to children. But are reasonable people always swayed by the stories they read in the newspapers? Or do they take a more level-headed standpoint, not believing everything they read?

To some extent, on the evidence of opinions obtained in this study, it appears that people while concerned, are not prepared to believe everything they are told. Around half did not think that the violence issue had been blown up out of proportion, perhaps reflecting earlier opinions about how serious an issue it was perceived to be. The remainder, however, either thought that it had been exaggerated or were not sure. Opinions were equally divided on whether newspapers usually exaggerate the effects TV violence can have on children (see Table 3.4).

Table 3.4 The violence issue in perspective

	Agree %	Neither %	Disagree %
The effects that TV violence can have on children are usually exaggerated by the newspapers	36	29	35
It is my opinion that the violence issue has been blown up out of all proportion	29	22	49

SOURCE: IBA/BARB

General opinions about violence on TV

The controversy surrounding the portrayal of violence on TV embodies many different worries and questions related to the possible social effects on audiences and to decisions governing what is permitted on screen and under what circumstances. One accusation often levelled against broadcasters is that there is simply too much violence on TV. When issued as a bland, unspecified statement, a typical finding is that most people will agree that there is. This 1986 IBA survey was no exception, as six out of ten respondents stated their agreement.

If we turn from the standard annual general survey to the results of more detailed questions explored through weekly omnibus surveys with a national opinion panel, a less extreme point of view emerges that while some violent programmes may be shown, they should be restricted to late at night, with the presumption that few children are likely to be watching them. Eight out of ten respondents agreed with this idea. A number of what we might call "socially responsible" opinions were given with regard to general notions about the showing of violence on TV. Most people, for example, were likely to agree with the statement that "there is too much violence on TV", and more than half also agreed that we would all be better off without violence on TV, since there is already enough in real life. There was no strong desire either to see violence on TV become more realistic. More than six out of ten rejected the wish to see programmes such as *The Sweeney* show more realistic forms of violence. Despite these cautious sentiments, however, relatively few respondents agreed with the stringent reflection that they themselves were adversely affected by TV violence, and opinions were divided on whether it was a sign of good sense and awareness to believe that television is harmful to people (see Table 3.5).

The six percent who are willing to admit that they may *sometimes* feel quite violent after watching crime programmes would amount to two million or so adults, by projection from the sample proportion to the whole population. It is important to recognise, however, that we are dealing here with personal claims about *feelings* which are to be distinguished from overt *behaviour*. Among those individuals who express some form of emotional arousal while watching crime programmes, there may be a substantial number who answer in this way because they have insight into their reactions and this insight would help to forestall any "translation" of such feelings into action. Although it was not included in this survey, it is in addition relevant to know whether, as a result of violent feelings supposedly aroused by exciting crime dramas on television, viewers then *act* violently. The possibility that some viewers may sometimes become aroused to anger through watching exciting crime drama is a finding which carries important implications, the meaning of which needs to be more clearly elaborated. In consequence, this and other supplementary questions designed to assess in more precise terms the feelings that are produced by television violence, what these feelings mean to viewers, and whether they ever give rise to behavioural reactions, are currently the subject of further study by the IBA. In addition, it is important not to ignore the possibility that there may be others who acknowledge violent feelings without having the ability to restrain themselves if circumstances on occasion provide the opportunity or provocation. *This group of individuals, probably small in numbers, nevertheless with their potential susceptibilities, remain in the minds of broadcasters as a responsibility about which they are concerned and aware.*

Table 3.5 Miscellaneous opinions about violence on TV

	Agree	Neither	Disagree
	%	%	%
TV programmes containing violence should be broadcast late at night	80	12	8
There are too many programmes on television that contain violence	60	21	19
We would be better off without violence on television; there is already enough in real life	55	24	21
I sometimes wish that violence in programmes (like The Sweeney) was more realistic	15	22	63
People who say that television is harmful to people don't know what they're talking about	32	33	35
Sometimes I can feel quite violent after watching crime programmes	6	7	87

SOURCE: IBA/BARB

Controls and warnings

Much of the adult concern over the showing of violence on TV rests with beliefs about the possible harms such content might do to children. However, not all programmes are designed for young audiences. There are programmes which are made for adult audiences that are perfectly suitable for mature viewers to watch, though not for children. Even among adult viewers, though, tastes can vary a lot. What may be found acceptable by one viewer may not be by another. There are various ways in which broadcasters can cope with this conflict of interests and tastes. Limits may be set on the times at which particular programmes are allowed to be broadcast. Programmes with potentially upsetting material may be preceded by a clear warning about its content, so that viewers who do not wish to see it can turn to a different channel or switch off altogether. Warnings may be provided in television guides or newspaper television listings, or they may, as they have in some experiments, be presented on screen for the duration of the programme. But what do the public think about these different methods of control or guidance?

Should potentially offending material of various sorts be shown at all? And if the answer to that question is yes, then how best can viewers be helped to decide for themselves whether or not to watch, when a potential conflict of acceptability may result from a particular programme being transmitted? A survey was carried out with a national viewing panel to find out. Attitudes concerning the depiction of lethal violence, explicit sex and foul language in documentaries and films or plays were investigated.

Attitude statements varied from outright rejection that a particular kind of content should ever be shown to the softer line that violence, sex or bad language are acceptable under certain circumstances. First we will

Table 3.6 Opinions concerning the showing of lethal violence on television

	Documentaries			Films/Plays		
	Agree %	Neither %	Dis-agree %	Agree %	Neither %	Dis-agree %
This kind of thing could be shown at any time or on any channel and leave it to people to *take care of themselves* by watching or not, as they feel fit	24	12	64	28	15	57
This kind of thing should *never be shown*	22	16	62	29	19	52
This kind of thing should be shown only on a *special channel* such as BBC2 or C4	39	18	43	35	18	47
This kind of thing should only be shown when there is a *published warning* in papers, TV/Radio Times	39	27	34	42	26	32
This kind of thing should only be shown if there is a *warning triangle* in the corner of the screen beforehand to let people know what may be coming	52	25	23	49	25	26
This kind of thing should only be shown if there is a *clear warning* announced on TV beforehand	75	13	12	64	18	18
This kind of thing should be shown only after a *time limit* such as 9 or 10 pm	81	8	11	73	11	16

SOURCE: IBA/BARB

look at the results for lethal violence. These are shown in Table 3.6. Most respondents were not of the opinion that "lethal violence" should never be shown, whether in films or in documentaries. More adhered to this opinion with respect to documentaries than for films or plays. There was no overwhelming support for restrictions of such content to certain channels, such as the two minority channels, BBC2 and Channel Four.

There was extensive support for time limit restrictions, however. More than eight out of ten supported the restriction of lethal violence to late-night viewing for documentaries, and more than seven out of ten did likewise with regard to films or plays. A majority of respondents endorsed the announcement of a clear warning before a potentially problematic programme, while there was less support for the usefulness of published warnings in newspapers or television guides. The idea of a warning symbol shown on screen for the duration of a programme requiring special discretion received support for factual and fictional programming from around half of respondents. Around half as many rejected this proposal. There was no more than modest support for letting viewers take care of themselves, while anything goes on the screen at any time. Although this report is concerned principally with opinions about violence on TV, it is of some interest to see how the public's opinions about sex and bad language on television compare. The character and distribution of these opinions are indicated in Tables 3.7 and 3.8.

There was widespread support for some restriction over when explicit sexual material should be permitted onto our television screens, whether in documentaries or in films and drama. This point of view did not extend to such extremes as total banishment of such content or restriction of it to special channels. On the other side of the coin, however, respondents did not for the most part believe that viewers should be left totally to their own devices without any guidance from broadcasters. It emerged that many respondents felt that some form of advance or continuous on-screen warning about the nature of programme content would be appropriate and useful in connection with the showing of explicit sexual content.

Opinions concerning the showing of bad language on television were distributed similarly to those concerning explicit sex. The main difference was that fewer respondents in general were in favour of programmes containing bad language compared with sex (or violence) under any circumstances.

To sum up, as far as the question of who should control the screening of violent, explicit sexual and "earthy" material is concerned, the public clearly take a middle view as to responsibility, and mark relatively minor distinctions as between types of material. That is to say, they reject the idea that the broadcasters should exercise rigid exclusive controls; they also reject the idea that the broadcaster should abandon all controls

(″leave it to the viewer″). Instead, people prefer to have a mixture of controls exercised by broadcasters and warnings giving initiative to themselves as well as to exercise self control based on effective information.

Table 3.7 Opinions concerning the showing of explicit sex on television

| | Documentaries | | | Films/Plays | | |
	Agree %	Neither %	Dis-agree %	Agree %	Neither %	Dis-agree %
This kind of thing could be shown at any time or on any channel and leave it to people to *take care of themselves* by watching or not, as they feel fit	25	13	62	26	14	60
This kind of thing should *never be shown*	26	19	55	30	19	51
This kind of thing should be shown only on a *special channel* such as BBC2 or C4	42	17	41	39	17	44
This kind of thing should only be shown when there is a *published warning* in papers, TV/Radio Times	40	25	35	45	24	31
This kind of thing should only be shown if there is a *warning triangle* in the corner of the screen beforehand to let people know what may be coming	51	24	25	52	23	25
This kind of thing should only be shown if there is a *clear warning* announced on TV beforehand	68	16	16	67	16	17
This kind of thing should be shown only after a *time limit* such as 9 or 10 pm	80	7	13	79	8	13

SOURCE: IBA/BARB

Table 3.8 Opinions concerning language on television

	Documentaries			Films/Plays		
	Agree %	Neither %	Dis-agree %	Agree %	Neither %	Dis-agree %
This kind of thing could be shown at any time or on any channel and leave it to people to *take care of themselves* by watching or not, as they feel fit	29	15	56	28	16	56
This kind of thing should *never be shown*	34	19	47	34	19	47
This kind of thing should be shown only on a *special channel* such as BBC2 or C4	34	19	47	34	19	47
This kind of thing should only be shown when there is a *published warning* in papers, TV/Radio Times	37	26	37	42	25	33
This kind of thing should only be shown if there is a *warning triangle* in the corner of the screen beforehand to let people know what may be coming	46	25	29	48	24	28
This kind of thing should only be shown if there is a *clear warning* announced on TV beforehand	62	17	21	61	19	20
This kind of thing should be shown only after a *time limit* such as 9 or 10 pm	68	13	19	70	13	17

SOURCE: IBA/BARB

The climate of violence, in viewers' experience on different channels

A major question examined in recent television research has been whether the amount of experience people have of the screen somehow conditions their views of what is on the screen – and of what exists in real life. Here, we shall examine just the first part of this question, as far as the violent contents of the screen can be described in a short questionnaire.

23

Table 3.9 Amount of viewing and opinions about violence shown on different television channels

		Heavy Viewers	Medium Viewers	Light Viewers	Aver-ages
Positive items		%	%	%	%
Violent programmes have	ITV	59	57	52	56
been kept to late hours	BBC1	64	59	47	57
	C4	58	51	44	51
	BBC2	59	55	48	54
Proportions of violent	ITV	57	53	44	51
programmes has	BBC1	60	58	44	54
been small	C4	51	49	43	48
	BBC2	58	59	51	56
Violence shown has	ITV	53	44	42	46
been necessary for	BBC1	55	44	41	47
the plots	C4	48	38	40	42
	BBC2	50	42	43	45
Enough information in	ITV	51	43	41	45
TV/Radio Times to	BBC1	51	43	41	45
inform viewers about	C4	44	37	38	40
violence	BBC2	47	42	39	43
Grand Total		865	774	698	780
Negative items		%	%	%	%
There have been too	ITV	56	53	46	52
few non-violent	BBC1	51	47	41	46
but exciting programmes	C4	44	38	29	37
	BBC2	41	37	26	35
Violence shown has	ITV	45	46	40	44
been getting tougher	BBC1	38	42	38	39
	C4	35	35	29	33
	BBC2	31	34	28	31
There have been	ITV	33	31	28	31
many violent films on:	BBC1	38	42	38	39
	C4	18	19	20	19
	BBC2	12	9	11	11
There have been	ITV	32	31	32	32
many violent series on:	BBC1	23	23	27	24
	C4	16	16	17	16
	BBC2	10	9	10	10
Grand Total		509	495	447	499

SOURCE: IBA/BARB

Viewers were asked first whether they watched less than two, more than four or an intermediate number of hours' television on an average day and qualified thereby as light, heavy and medium viewers. Each set of viewers then answered the same descriptions of violence as it was considered to be handled on each channel. There were four positive items and four negative ones in their general tone and implications, and it can be seen that these differences in tone are reflected in different patterns of responses.

The first result is that the proportions of people agreeing with the positive items were overall substantially greater than the proportions agreeing with the negative descriptions. This general conclusion over-rides questions affecting particular channels or degrees of experience among viewers.

Next, we may observe that heavy viewers have a relatively greater positive differential than have light viewers. That is to say that the difference between tendencies to agree to positive and negative statements is large among heavy viewers; this difference is not so large among light viewers. The light viewers still have an overall positive inclination, but not by such a great margin as have the heavy viewers.

Among the positive items three channels emerge with approximately equal measures of endorsement; one channel is slightly behind, and this is Channel 4. This lower level of endorsement is not likely to be simply because of lower familiarity with Channel 4 – as the next comparison indicates.

Among the negative items the channel with largest proportion of endorsements has been ITV – then BBC1 and then Channel 4. BBC2 comes in for the lowest level of criticism (by endorsement of negative items). The fact that Channel 4 is not last in rank here discourages the view that it is unfamiliarity that left this channel in last place on the positive list items.

The link between weight of viewing and tendency to agree with statements exists both for negative and for positive items. This takes force away from any simple inference that heavy viewing makes viewers more tolerant – or that more tolerant people view more. Part of the problem with these results is likely to do with a general tendency to "yea-say" – some people call themselves heavier viewers and are also more likely to agree with attitude statements, whether they are consistent or even opposing in meaning. Yet, as has been mentioned, there is still a greater 'positive bias' amongst heavy viewers, and there may be some reinforcement here whereby those who think well of television – including the way it deals with violence – watch more of the screen.

Escaping the general tendencies described in the above paragraphs are the items saying there have been many violent films, or series on each channel; for these items, weight of viewing experience makes no difference – all are agreed to the same albeit relatively low extent, about the volume of violence. The main difference in implied criticism is opened up by the item exploring the need, or desire for "non-violent but exciting programmes".

TV violence and children

Earlier surveys indicated that in general terms people say they are concerned about television violence, especially for the harm it may do to young viewers. When television is publicly criticised for its violent content, moreover, it is not uncommon for specific programmes to be singled out for special treatment. In the next section, therefore, we report results from surveys of public opinion about particular television series which have often been singled out for concern. Some of these series are British productions, while others are imports to our television screens from the United States. All have proved to be popular with viewers in terms of the audiences they have attracted.

We begin our analysis by examining adult viewers' perceptions of the possible harms that might fall on children who watch certain series whose dramatic themes in the main centre on crime and law enforcement and where violence often plays a prominent role in the storyline. The following results derive from a series of surveys with a national television opinion panel where panellists who in their viewing diaries indicated they had watched that week's episode, answered further questions about the programme.

We first of all asked respondents whether they watched a programme with their children (if they had children), and if so, whether they thought their youngsters may have been harmed by it, or whether it was seen as being harmless entertainment. We asked also about the age of children with whom a programme was watched and for estimates of the likely harm that may have been caused to children of different ages up to 15 years by the programme in question.

Nine television series are featured here. From Britain, we asked about *Dempsey and Makepeace* and *Minder*. And from the United States, we asked about *The A-Team, Knight Rider, Starsky and Hutch, Magnum, Miami Vice, The Equalizer* and *Hill Street Blues*.

On average, about one in five (22%) respondents claimed to have watched particular episodes from these series with their children. Each week only those respondents who indicated in their viewing diaries that they watched that week's episode answered any further questions about the programme. Those who said they watched with children went on to answer two more questions. First, how old were the children with whom they watched; and second, did they think the programme had done their children any harm?

Extent of watching TV drama series with children

There were variations across series in the extent to which parents indicated watching with their children (see Table 3.10). The programme that more respondents than for any other said they had watched with children was *The A-Team*. Four out of ten said they watched this show with their children during the week of that particular survey. Among those individuals who had children at all, however, the proportion who watched *The A-Team* with their youngsters (71%) was much higher.

The programme respondents were least likely to watch with their children was *Hill Street Blues*. Fewer than one in ten said they watched this show with their youngsters during the survey week. This amounted to around one in seven adults with children (14%).

Another show which is very popular with young viewers, and which is specially targetted for them, is *Knight Rider*. Two out of three parents (66%) watched this programme with their children.

It is borne in mind as well, that some programmes are likely to be watched by children without their parents; this was not asked about explicitly here, but we can infer from the subsequent questions on parents' views about the possible influence on their children that those series that are considered more likely to be harmless are the ones which children are allowed to watch unattended.

Among the more adult-oriented series from the United States, which tend to be broadcast later in the evening, fewer respondents claimed to watch these programmes with children. During separate survey weeks, around one in four panellists reported watching *Starsky and Hutch* and *Magnum* with children. Around four out of ten (42%) parents watched *Starsky and Hutch* with their children, while just over half (51%) reported doing so with *Magnum*. The two newest American crime-detective series were less widely watched by adult viewers with their children present. Fewer than one in three (29%) of panellists with children watched *Miami Vice* with their youngsters, while even fewer (26%) watched *The Equalizer* with their children.

Turning to the two British series, just under one in three parents (31%) on the panel watched *Minder* with their children, while a somewhat larger proportion (41%) watched *Dempsey and Makepeace* with their children. These figures are recalculated from those in the table, to focus only on those adults who have children. Childless people, on average, constitute about 49 percent of the audience for any one of these series, with little variation. Among those panellists with children, 15 percent, on average, watched any of the first four listed series with their children, while 27 percent, on average, watched any of the second set of series with their children.

Among those panellists who watched crime series with their children,

Table 3.10 Parents opinions about the impact of selected television series on their children

	Hill Street Blues	Miami Vice	Dempsey and Makepeace	The Equaliser	Starsky and Hutch	Knight Rider	Minder	The A Team	Magnum
Base sizes	703	476	504	832	184	196	527	582	457
Did you watch this programme with your children	%	%	%	%	%	%	%		%
Yes	7	14	19	15	24	32	16	40	24
No	43	35	27	41	33	16	36	16	23
No children	49	51	54	44	43	52	48	43	54
Base sizes (Those who said YES)	49	66	96	125	44	63	84	233	110
	%	%	%	%	%	%	%	%	%
How old were the children who watched with you									
0-5	10	12	13	12	20	20	15	39	39
6-10	16	10	20	13	20	20	9	31	35
11-15	74	78	66	75	61	60	76	30	27
May have been harmful for:									
0-5	47	38	37	39	20	17	8	14	9
6-10	40	44	27	22	9	11	14	5	8
11-15	13	6	11	11	10	4	11	8	5
Not sure, for:									
0-5	42	37	30	23	23	30	18	13	12
6-10	38	29	25	14	25	19	17	11	9
11-15	34	16	12	19	9	11	14	9	9
Harmless entertainment for:									
0-5	10	26	33	39	57	53	74	73	79
6-10	23	28	48	64	66	70	69	84	84
11-15	53	78	77	70	81	85	75	83	86

SOURCE: IBA/BARB

further questioning was aimed at finding out how old those children were. As Table 3.10 shows, for nearly all series, with just two exceptions, viewing was done with children aged between 11 and 15 years. Except for *The A-Team* and *Knight Rider*, relatively few parents watched adult-oriented crime series with children aged under 10 years.

Beliefs about effects of TV drama series on children

Among those panellists who reported watching particular programmes with children within each of the three age groups, we asked what effect they thought each show might have had on their youngsters. As Table 3.10 indicates, there was considerable variation in opinions across television series. With respect first of all to children aged up to five, around three out of four parents felt that programmes such as *The A-Team*, *Knight Rider* and *Minder* were harmless entertainment. More than half felt that *Starsky and Hutch* and *Magnum* were unlikely to be harmful to this youngest age group. With regard to the first set of four series, however, far fewer parents were sure that these programmes were safe viewing fare for very young children. Nearly half of those who watched *Hill Street Blues* with children under five present, felt that that show may have been harmful. And nearly four out of ten who watched *The Equalizer*, *Miami Vice* or *Dempsey and Makepeace* with children from this youngest age group felt that these programmes may have been harmful to their children.

As we step up to the next age group, 6 to 10-year olds, the proportions of parents who felt that no harm was done by crime series increased across eight out of the nine series on which surveys were done. More than eight out of ten believed that *The A-Team* and *Knight Rider* did no harm to this middle-age range. And more than six out of ten believed that no harm was done either by series such as *Minder, Starsky and Hutch* and *The Equalizer*. In the case of all the above series, except *The Equalizer*, among the remaining respondents, most were uncertain about the effects one way or the other. More than one in five parents who watched *The Equalizer* with their 6 to 10-year olds felt that it may have been harmful to them. For the other series, relatively small percentages endorsed this opinion. There was somewhat more widespread concern about *Dempsey and Makepeace*, although far more parents thought that it was harmless rather than harmful for their 6 to 10-year olds. Most concern of all was revealed with regard to American imports, *Miami Vice* and *Hill Street Blues*, where panellists who perceived them as harmful outnumbered those who thought they were harmless for the 6 to 10s.

With the oldest children about whom we questioned parents, practically all the series were seen mostly as harmless entertainment. Parents were still reasonably cautious about *Hill Street Blues*, though more than half thought it was unlikely to harm their teenage children, while the percentage who felt that it might was much reduced compared with younger age groups.

Concluding Remarks

In this chapter we have presented the findings from a number of nationwide surveys conducted in the United Kingdom in which opinions regarding the portrayal of violence on TV have been investigated. Opinions were found to vary quite a lot with the types of questions being asked and with the types of content being asked about. This in itself is a very important finding because it shows that public concerns about TV violence can be effectively measured only by taking into account a wide range of opinions about the many different ways in which violence can be and is portrayed on TV.

Agreement with statements about possible harmful effects of TV violence outweighed disagreement, while agreement with statements about the harmlessness of TV violence was less frequent. Few respondents felt that TV violence actually has any beneficial effects. These findings suggest that people hold some concerns about violence on TV and believe that it is more likely to do harm than to be benign. However, to consider these attitudes on their own would fail to provide a complete picture of what the public believes about TV violence.

There was widespread feeling, for instance, that parents should take greater control over what their children watch, particularly with regard to programmes containing violence. Parents should, it is widely believed, steer their children clear of TV violence for as long as possible. Perhaps one reason for wanting to see greater protection of children and responsible parental control over youngsters' viewing is the belief that children are not as discriminating as adults. Many respondents in our surveys believed that children are often unable to distinguish when violence on TV is real or make-believe. There was a widely held opinion too that TV violence might give children the misleading impression that murder and mayhem are commonplace in real life. It is interesting though that many respondents felt that to remove violence from TV altogether would present too rosy a picture of what the world is like. Thus, despite opinions indicating a level of concern about showing violence on TV, members of the public are also aware of an important role played by television in reflecting events that occur in reality and in showing the way the world really is. This perception is reflected in other opinions we obtained from our survey respondents which we mention again below.

The need to vary the kinds of questions that are asked in order to derive a complete picture of what people really think about TV is reinforced by our findings concerning opinions towards the way the issue is covered by the press. Our respondents were equally likely to agree or disagree that the press exaggerate the effects that TV violence can have on children, while disagreements outweighed agreements on the opinion that the issue has been blown up out of proportion. Thus, people believe that this is an important issue deserving of media coverage and discussion, but they are not entirely convinced by the line taken by many press stories about how youngsters have been affected by violence on TV.

A majority of individuals across the country felt that there were too many violence-containing programmes on TV, and more than half felt that we would be better off without violence on TV. But while, as a matter of taste, violence was not widely favoured, respondents in our surveys did not feel overwhelmingly that TV violence had a harmful impact. The vast majority dismissed any suggestion that they themselves were made to feel violent by watching crime programmes.

Although respondents, when asked outright, tended to endorse the view that there is "too much violence on TV", the majority also reject the opinion that violence should never be shown. Instead, there is an acceptance of the necessity to include violence sometimes, whether in fictional or factual programming, to tell a story or to get a point across. However, viewers do ask for limits to be placed on when such programmes are broadcast and favour the idea of more information or guidance from broadcasters (in the form of warning symbols on screen and more detail about programmes in TV magazines and newspapers) about the content of programmes.

There is a common belief that the more people see TV violence the more accustomed or habituated to it they become. Regular exposure to violence on the screen can condition in viewers a greater acceptance of that sort of content. Comparisons we make between the opinions of heavy and light viewers, however, indicated that although there was a tendency for heavy viewers to endorse positive statements about TV violence more often than did light viewers, the same pattern of responding held with regard to negative attitudes about violence in programmes. This may indicate that those who think well of TV violence watch more programmes, and they then become more positively disposed towards violent portrayals. Alternatively, it could be that individuals who report watching a lot of television have a tendency to agree with attitude-statements of any kind.

Finally, concern about the impact of violence-containing programmes on their audience has been particularly focused with respect to children. Our surveys have revealed, however, that parents extensively watch a number of heavily criticised British and American crime-drama series with their children, and in most cases, few acknowledged that these programmes may have had a negative influence on their children. Where concern was voiced by sizeable minorities (which was relatively rare) it was usually about very young children (up to the age of six years) when watching more realistic, contemporary crime series not designed for that age group anyway.

CHAPTER FOUR

OPINIONS ABOUT VIOLENCE IN UK CRIME SERIES

Opinions about UK crime series

Criticisms of television violence are often levelled against particular television series. Television's crime drama genre is usually in the firing line more than any other, with storylines which regularly feature violent criminal behaviour, and leading characters who frequently use violent means to overcome obstacles. The lessons that these programmes might teach children have been of particular public concern. If they see their favourite television characters using violence in various situations, might young viewers become inclined to do likewise when faced with similar problems? This is one question which is routinely asked. Apart from influencing children's behaviour, there have been worries that TV violence may frighten youngsters or produce distorted impressions about the world, in particular in connection with the perceived level of criminal activity.

Concerns about possible effects of violent television programmes are not the only ones broadcasters have to contend with though. There is also the important matter of public taste and ensuring that the things shown in programmes do not offend viewers. Some viewers do find violence offensive, even though they may not be changed by it in any psychological sense. While a great deal of research has been carried out on the impact of TV violence on the attitudes and behaviour of viewers, far less systematic work has investigated what television audiences think about the content of popular programmes. In particular, in the context of the present discussion, what do viewers think about the violence they see in TV crime drama series? Do they feel that the amount of violence shown is excessive? Do they like the way law enforcers and criminals are shown? And to what extent are such opinions constant across series? We have seen in the previous chapter that crime drama series fall into two broad groupings – one exemplified by four series which tend to be watched less with children and which have larger numbers saying they may be harmful for young children; and one set, represented by five examples here, which relatively few people consider are harmful for children and which are more extensively watched with the children. In what follows in this and the next chapter the opinions about British and US crime series are looked at separately, but neither group is large enough to, or is purported to, represent the whole body of British or US programming in this genre.

We begin by examining opinions concerning a number of British crime drama series. We report opinions on five series in all. We make comparisons between them on a constant set of attitude statements. In the comparative analysis, we look at audience opinions of *Bergerac*, *Juliet Bravo*, *Cats Eyes*, *The Bill* and *Dempsey and Makepeace*. Here we asked members of a national television opinion panel who had watched the episode from the series broadcast during the week of survey about their perceptions of the portrayals of the police and criminals, about the perceived suitability of these programmes for children, and finally we asked respondents to give several miscellaneous evaluations of each series.

Perceptions of violence in UK crime series

Perceptions of violence concerned whether viewers felt that a programme happened to be the most violent series on television, or whether they

Table 4.1 Perceptions of violence in UK crime series

	Bergerac %	Juliet Bravo %	Cats Eyes %	The Bill %	Dempsey and Makepeace %
There are many more violent programmes than ... on TV at the moment	93	95	87	84	84
From what I have seen, the violence on ... is often necessary to the story	66	74	62	74	60
... features too many extreme forms of violence for my liking	6	4	10	10	18

felt that there are many other more violent series, whether the violence shown on screen was always necessary to the story, and whether in general a series contained too many extreme forms of violence for personal tastes. As Table 4.1 indicates, more than eight out of ten viewers of each series believed there were many more violent series on television than the one in question. This was felt to be the case most often for *Bergerac* and *Juliet Bravo*. More than six out of ten viewers of these series felt that from what they had seen the violence was often necessary to the story. More than seven out of ten thought this was true for *Juliet Bravo* and *The Bill*. Few respondents agreed that these series were far too violent for their liking. At least three times as many *Dempsey and Makepeace* viewers felt that the show was too violent as did viewers of *Bergerac* and *Juliet Bravo*.

Perceptions of police and criminals in UK crime series

The extent to which viewers felt that the use of violence by the police in these series was justified varied quite a lot from one programme to the next (see Table 4.2). Seven out of ten thought that this was true of *Juliet Bravo*, compared with nearly six out of ten for *The Bill*, just over one in two for *Bergerac* and less than one in two for *Cats Eyes*. Fully justified police violence was perceived to occur least often in *Dempsey and*

Table 4.2 Perceptions of police and criminals in UK crime series

	Bergerac %	Juliet Bravo %	Cats Eyes %	The Bill %	Dempsey and Makepeace %
I think that the use of violence by the police in ... is nearly always fully justified	53	70	49	58	40
The police in real life would never behave like ... does	28	17	31	18	51
The police in ... are often far more violent than they need to be	10	5	16	15	35
... shows the police as too trigger happy	8	7	18	12	47
... shows the police in a bad light	6	6	*	12	22
... portrays the behaviour of criminals unrealistically	19	13	25	14	28

*Item not included

Makepeace. The perceived realism of the police varied across series too, but in general relatively few respondents accepted that these series gave unrealistic portrayals of police behaviour. The series perceived as least realistic was *Dempsey and Makepeace*. There was little feeling that the police in these dramas were usually more violent than they needed to be. This was especially true of *Juliet Bravo*. The police were most often seen as unnecessarily violent in *Dempsey and Makepeace*, but then by just over one in three viewers of the programme. The police were not seen as being too trigger happy by many viewers, nor were the police thought to be shown in a bad light. The exception to this rule, once again, was *Dempsey and Makepeace*. Nearly half the viewers of this programme felt that the police in it were too trigger happy. Criminals were also seen as being portrayed fairly realistically; only about one in five viewers of these series on average felt that criminals were portrayed unrealistically. The least realistic criminal portrayals (in line with perceptions of the police too) were perceived to occur in *Dempsey and Makepeace*.

Children and UK crime series

The perceived suitability of these programmes for children varied a great deal across the series (see Table 4.3). More than seven out of ten felt that *Juliet Bravo* is suitable for children to watch, even though many viewers felt that the series would be taken seriously by young viewers. Only one in ten said that this programme was not suitable for family viewing.

Rather more serious views were held about the other three series. Just under one in two felt that *Bergerac* is suitable for children, while just over four in ten agreed with this sentiment for *Dempsey and Makepeace* and *Cats Eyes*, and just one in three for *The Bill*. Despite this, viewers more often felt that *Bergerac* and *Cats Eyes* would not be taken seriously by children than they did for *Juliet Bravo*, or for *The Bill*. *The Bill* was

Table 4.3 Children and UK crime series

	Bergerac %	Juliet Bravo %	Cats Eyes %	The Bill %	Dempsey and Makepeace %
... is suitable for children to watch	47	72	41	33	44
... is not likely to be taken seriously by children	40	23	47	27	42
... is not suitable for family viewing	12	10	13	26	22

perceived most often to be unsuitable for family viewing. This series was scheduled after 9.00 p.m., however, outside of family viewing time during that period of the evening when programmes suitable for adult audiences are broadcast.

Evaluations of UK crime series

Further general evaluations revealed that only a minority of viewers thought that the storylines of these series tended to be repetitive; this was true more of *Bergerac* and *Cats Eyes* than of *Juliet Bravo* and *The Bill* however. Few viewers thought that these series were aimed at the American market, though *Dempsey and Makepeace* and *Cats Eyes* were perceived to adhere more to this style than any of the others. And few viewers said they would be glad to see any of these series taken off the screen.

Table 4.4 Evaluations of UK crime series

	Bergerac %	Juliet Bravo %	Cats Eyes %	The Bill %	Dempsey and Makepeace %
The storyline in ... is much the same every week	27	18	31	18	37
... is clearly designed to appeal to the American market	13	7	28	14	47
I would be glad to see ... taken off the screen	7	5	14	12	8

Concluding remarks

In this chapter our focus has been on opinions concerning a selection of British-made fictional, crime-drama series. It is designed to provide some broad indication of what viewers think about the violence, crime and law enforcement aspects of these TV series. There are advantages to asking viewers about TV violence in the context of particular programmes they have actually seen. For one thing, they can base their opinions on concrete examples of violent portrayals involving characters and settings with which they have some degree of familiarity. When asking viewers for opinions about the general concept of violence on TV, as is so typical of many surveys, one can never be sure how these opinions are formulated.

Are they based on specific examples of violence viewers can remember from a recent episode of a single TV series, or from several episodes in the same series? In each of our surveys, only respondents who indicated in their viewing diaries that they had watched that week's episode from a particular TV series were directed to provide additional opinions about it.

In the last chapter, we noted widespread agreement with statements proposing that television contains excessive amounts of violence. In connection with particular TV series, however, this sort of attitude was less commonplace. Violence is perpetrated by different types of characters on TV, who, within the context of particular storylines, have different motives or reasons for their aggressive actions. An important element likely to affect viewers' judgements about TV violence therefore is the nature of the aggressor. In TV crime series, conflicts usually revolve around the actions of law breakers and law-enforcers. We asked our respondents to give their opinions about both of these groups, with our main focus being on perceptions of portrayals of the police.

Our findings revealed that although sizeable proportions of respondents perceived the use of violence by fictional police to be nearly always justified, the extent to which this opinion was held varied considerably across TV series and was not always a majority opinion. However, in most cases, few respondents felt that fictional police were more violent than they needed to be nor were they perceived to be 'trigger happy'. Fictional portrayals of the police were generally not perceived by the majority to reflect the behaviour of real life police. The portrayal of criminal behaviour in contrast, was perceived by most viewers to be realistic.

With all except one of our selected TV crime series, there were reservations about the suitability of these programmes for children. Many respondents felt that children were likely to take these programmes seriously. This may be why there is some indication that the real cause of concern may be that children may watch TV crime series on their own without the company of an adult, since most respondents felt that these series are suitable for family viewing.

General evaluations of UK crime series were, on the whole, positive. Storylines were perceived to contain variety and few respondents said they would be glad to see any of these series taken off the screen; and this opinion prevailed despite earlier reservations about the suitability of these programmes for young viewers.

CHAPTER FIVE

OPINIONS ABOUT VIOLENCE IN US CRIME SERIES

Opinions about US crime series

Crime drama series imported from the United States have been a
prominent and popular part of the television schedules in this country for
many years. Some of these programmes have been severely criticised
however, both in the USA and in Britain, for their violence content. Public
anxieties have been sharpened particularly because these programmes
tend to attract many young viewers. In this chapter we examine what
audiences think about the violence in these programmes. The research
runs a parallel course to that reported in the last chapter. We begin by
making comparisons between attitudes towards three American crime
series, *Knight Rider*, *Magnum* and *Murder She Wrote*. Next we look at
similar attitudes towards the latest popular American crime-fighting
import, *The Equalizer*, which actually stars a British actor. Finally, we
examine a slightly more extensive set of opinions towards one of the
most popular action-adventure series with young people over the last few
years, *The A-Team*. As in the last chapter, comparisons between series are
made along four major categories of opinion: perceptions of violence in
the series, perceptions of the portrayal of the police (or law enforcers)
and criminals, suitability for children and general evaluations.

Perceptions of violence in US crime series

As Table 5.1 shows, more than nine out of ten viewers of these series
among a national television opinion panel, felt that there are many other

more violent programmes on television than each of these series. There is a possible logical paradox inherent in these results; for not only does each particular judgement imply that a particular series is not so violent, it also suggests that other series are more violent; but when other series are investigated none of them is acknowledged to be the location of greatest violence. It is known from other research that viewers do not generally patronise just one series, but support several series within a genre, so it is unlikely that people are saying that 'other series' are more violent just because they are unfamiliar with them. It is more likely that the question is being treated simply as an assessment of the level of violence the series is felt to show and the answers are reasonably interpreted as implying that people do not consider any of these series to be unduly violent.

There was less widespread agreement over whether the violence shown in these series was always necessary to the story. Around six out of ten felt that this was true for *Knight Rider* and *Magnum*, whilst just under half felt that it was true of *Murder She Wrote*. Fewer than one in ten viewers of these programmes felt that they were too violent for personal tastes.

Table 5.1 Perceptions of violence in US crime series

	Knight Rider %	Magnum %	Murder She Wrote %
There are many more violent programmes than ... on TV at the moment	91	93	93
From what I have seen, the violence on ... is often necessary to the story	58	60	49
... features too many extreme forms of violence for my liking	8	8	7

Perceptions of police and criminals in US crime series

Fewer than half the viewers questioned about these American crime series felt that the police or law enforcers in them were usually justified in their use of violence (see Table 5.2). Portrayals of the police were not widely perceived as realistic, though just four out of ten viewers actually rejected their authenticity outright. Although law enforcers may not always have been justified in their use of violence, they were not perceived to be too violent too often. Fewer than one in five viewers thought that the police in these series were too trigger happy. Just one in three viewers felt that criminals were portrayed unrealistically across these three series.

Table 5.2 Perceptions of police and criminals in US crime series

	Knight Rider %	Magnum %	Murder She Wrote %
I think that the use of violence by the police in ... is nearly always fully justified	43	47	49
The police in real life would never behave like ... does	41	41	38
The police in ... are often far more violent than they need to be	15	16	9
... shows the police as too trigger happy	18	18	9
... portrays the behaviour of criminals unrealistically	31	33	31

Children and US crime series

A majority of viewers believed that these series were suitable for children, while around half also felt that these programmes are not likely to be taken seriously by young viewers (see Table 5.3). Few viewers agreed that the series were not suitable for family viewing. There were some differences between series, however, and these are worth looking at further.

Knight Rider was most often perceived to be suitable for children by quite a large margin. The next most suitable was *Magnum* with *Murder She Wrote* finishing up some distance behind. The few items examined here turn out to be much more widely judged as suitable for children to watch, than are the examples of UK crime series (see Table 5.3).

Table 5.3 Children and US crime series

	Knight Rider %	Magnum %	Murder She Wrote %
... is suitable for children to watch	75	60	51
... is not likely to be taken seriously by children	46	52	50
... is not suitable for family viewing	4	8	12

Evaluations of US crime series

Knight Rider was more often perceived to have a repetitive storyline than the other two series (see Table 5.4). Just under one in two viewers questioned here felt that the storyline was very similar from one week to the next, while around four out of ten endorsed this opinion for *Magnum* and *Murder She Wrote*. All three series were perceived to be designed to appeal mainly to the American market, but not by a majority of their viewers. Few respondents actually said they would be glad to see any of these series removed from the screen.

Table 5.4 Evaluations of US crime series

	Knight Rider %	Magnum %	Murder She Wrote %
The storyline in ... is much the same every week	48	39	44
... is clearly designed to appeal to the American market	45	41	37
I would be glad to see ... taken off the screen	11	10	6

The Equalizer

The Equalizer is one of the latest crime drama series from the United States starring an English actor, Edward Woodward. Each week the story revolves around the good deeds of Woodward who plays a character called McCall, an ex-CIA agent who now spends his time helping the poor and weak who are put upon by the powerful and evil criminal elements in New York. McCall is a highly trained professional who is prepared to use violent means to overcome the bad guys, though only when absolutely necessary (which occurs in nearly every episode). But what do viewers feel about this new television hero? The opinions below have been recorded from those who had seen an episode of the series in one particular week.

Perceptions of violence

Around three out of four viewers of the show felt that there are many programmes more violent than *The Equalizer*. Six out of ten said it was not too violent for their taste. However, relatively few agreed that the violence was always necessary to the plot. Just over one in five thought that it was, while nearly twice as many disagreed.

Table 5.5 Perceptions of violence in The Equalizer

	Agree %	Neither %	Disagree %
There are many programmes more violent than The Equalizer on TV at the moment	74	21	5
It is not too violent for my liking	61	21	18
From what I have seen, the violence is often necessary to the storyline	23	32	45

Perceptions of police and criminals

There was no general consensus of opinion about the portrayal of the police in this programme. Around one in three felt that the police usually exhibited caution in their use of guns, while one in four disagreed. There was a similar distribution of responses to the perceived realism of the police. On balance, viewers felt that the police were shown in a good light by this series, although nearly half of viewers were undecided. There were mixed opinions also about the justification for violence when used by the police. Similar proportions of viewers agreed and disagreed on this issue. More than half of viewers thought that *The Equalizer* portrays the behaviour of criminals realistically, while just one in ten disagreed.

Table 5.6 Perceptions of police and criminals in The Equalizer

	Agree %	Neither %	Disagree %
It portrays the behaviour of criminals realistically	56	34	10
The programme shows the police in a good light	37	49	14
The police in real life might on occasion behave as they do in *The Equalizer*	33	37	30
The programme portrays the police as very cautious in the way they use guns and weapons	32	43	25
It portrays police activities in an unrealistic light	31	44	25
I think that the use of violence by the police in *The Equalizer* is seldom fully justified	26	47	27

Suitability for children

Half the viewers of *The Equalizer* in this survey felt that the programme was not suitable for children, while one in three did not think it was appropriate for the whole family either. Substantially more viewers found the show acceptable for family viewing than for children only, perhaps implying that it is all right for older children when viewing with their parents, but not for children watching on their own or for very young viewers under any circumstances. Just over one in three thought the show would be taken seriously by children, with slightly fewer disagreeing about this.

Table 5.7 Children and The Equalizer

	Agree %	Neither %	Disagree %
It is not a programme that is suitable for children	50	28	22
It is suitable for family viewing	38	29	33
It is likely to be taken seriously by children	38	27	28

Evaluation of the series

A substantial majority of viewers thought that *The Equalizer* was different from run-of-the-mill American crime series. More than six out of ten also said they would be sorry to see it taken off and felt that there is quite a bit of variation in the storyline from week to week.

Table 5.8 Evaluation of The Equalizer

	Agree %	Neither %	Disagree %
It is different from a lot of American cop series we see on TV these days	84	10	6
I would be sorry to see this taken off the screen	63	22	15
The storyline varies quite a lot from week to week	61	21	18

The A-Team

Another show that has been singled out for criticism by anti-television violence campaigners is *The A-Team*. This is such a familiar series and has had so much written about it that an extended and individually-tailored set of questions was designed to probe perceptions and feelings about it in more detail. Survey results reported in an earlier chapter indicated what parents who watched this series with their children thought its impact on young viewers might be. Given the early hour at which this programme is usually transmitted (5.35 pm on Saturdays) it is of special interest to know just what adult viewers think about this show, given the large numbers of children who are known to watch it.

We conducted two nationwide surveys with a television opinion panel in each of which viewers of that week's episode from the series were asked what they felt about the programme, its characters, storyline, violence in the show, and its suitability for children. The results indicated that viewers generally hold *The A-Team* in high regard and do not on the whole believe it does any real harm to young viewers (this corresponds well with what was reported in Table 3.10).

The characters in *The A-Team* are offbeat and viewers tended to evaluate them very favourably. As Table 5.9 below shows, between eight

Table 5.9 Perceptions of The A-Team characters

	Agree %	Neither %	Disagree %
Survey 1			
Crazy antics of The A-Team make the show entertaining	75	15	10
The members of The A-Team are all really nice people	68	21	11
The characters in The A-Team are very funny	46	32	22
Survey 2			
The A-Team members are basically good	85	12	3
The A-Team are very creative in the way they solve problems they get into	70	21	9
The A-Team don't care what methods they use to get even with their enemies	56	22	22
The A-Team members are basically bad	6	8	86

and nine out of ten viewers thought that *The A-Team* members are basically good, while very few thought they were in any way bad. For three out of four viewers the antics of *The A-Team* are what make the show so entertaining. For most viewers, the team are very nice people, who are also creative in the way they get out of tricky situations. However, more than half thought that *The A-Team* do not care which methods they use to get even with their enemies, although one in five disagreed with this view. This might indicate that although *The A-Team* are a law unto themselves in many respects, they do have a code of practice; they are honourable and do not go over the top unless it is really called for. A sizeable proportion of viewers thought that the members of *The A-Team* are very funny, and the show does have a strong comic element.

Viewers were asked about the violence in the show (Table 5.10). Nearly seven out of ten viewers said they were not bothered by all the guns and explosions which characterise the programme. For more than six out of ten the violence in the show was unreal, and few viewers disagreed with this. In addition, more than half claimed that because of the way the show is acted, it is not really violent at all. Again relatively few disagreed. Thus,

Table 5.10 Perceptions of violence in the A-Team

	Agree %	Neither %	Disagree %
Survey 1			
The use of violence by The A-Team is always justified	46	34	20
The members of The A-Team really enjoy being violent	27	25	48
There is too much extreme violence such as explosions on The A-Team	27	23	50
The A-Team is the most violent programme on television	11	20	69
Survey 2			
I am not bothered by all the guns and explosives going off	68	16	16
The violence in the programme is unreal	64	23	13
Because of the way it is acted, this show is not really violent at all	56	27	17
There is too much firing of guns and blowing up of cars and buildings	40	22	38
The violence in the programme is very real	17	21	62

there was net agreement with favourable or positive remarks about the show.

On the other side of the coin, we gave respondents a number of negative statements about the content of the show. These statements were designed to assess whether viewers felt there was too much violence in the show. On the whole, they did not think that there was, although over one quarter of respondents did feel that there was too much violence in the programme and that the stars did really enjoy being violent.

Just over one in four agreed that there is too much violence in *The A-Team*, but one in two rejected this opinion. Four out of ten felt there is too much firing of guns and blowing up of cars and buildings, while a similar proportion disagreed. The remainder were uncertain. Fewer than one in five thought that the violence in the show is very real, while over six out of ten rejected this proposition. Finally, around one in ten rated *The A-Team* as the most violent programme on television, while just under seven out of ten disagreed outright with this valuation.

Understandably, some people are concerned about the impact of the show on children. *The A-Team* is very popular with young viewers and there has been a deliberate attempt by the producers to emphasise the affinity certain of the characters in the show, especially Mr T, have with children. In both surveys, viewers were asked whether they thought *The A-Team* was potentially harmful for young viewers or simply harmless fun which they could enjoy without suffering any negative side effects.

Table 5.11 shows the results. On questions such as whether the show is broadcast too early, is bad for children and, in the case of Mr T specifically, is likely to frighten them, the vast majority of adult viewers indicated disagreement. Indeed more than seven out of ten viewers of the show rejected each of these potential harms. Less than one in six were prepared to accept the existence of any of them. The same pattern of results emerged for opinions such as *The A-Team* sets bad examples of how to behave for children and that shows like this should not be broadcast so early. (At the time of the survey, the series was transmitted at 5.35 p.m. on Saturdays.) Around six out of ten viewers did not accept either of these points of view, while most of those remaining were unsure. Most viewers recognised that no one gets hurt in the show, and more than half agreed that it is utterly fantastic, much like a cartoon in its style.

We probed further for viewers perceptions of the characters and storylines in *The A-Team*. A number of clear opinions about the programme emerged (see Table 5.12). For most viewers, the good guys and the bad guys were clearly distinguished and the bad guys usually got just what they deserved at the end of the show. The storyline was seen as being very predictable, and this probably accounts in part for its perceived suitability for children. Regular viewers of the show know the

Table 5.11 Perceived harmfulness or harmlessness for children

	Agree %	Neither %	Disagree %
Survey 1			
Harmfulness			
5.30 is too early to show The A-Team	15	14	71
The A-Team is very bad for children	11	12	72
Mr T is likely to frighten children	10	11	79
Harmlessness			
Few children take The A-Team seriously	51	30	19
The A-Team is really a children's programme	51	23	26
The A-Team is more like a cartoon than action-adventure	34	23	43
Survey 2			
Harmfulness			
The A-Team set bad examples of how to behave for young children	17	28	58
Programmes like this should not be shown so early in the evening	14	20	66
Harmlessness			
No one really gets hurt in the show	78	13	9
The show is utterly fantastic, like a cartoon	53	23	24

format and how things will turn out in the end. And clearly this is not disliked by viewers who are less strongly in favour of changes to the structure such as making things more difficult for *The A-Team* to win. This idea was accepted by a large minority of viewers, but many others either did not like it or were uncertain. There were mixed opinions on whether the show has now become too repetitive. The conclusion to be reached from this is probably that loyal viewers like the show the way it is and enjoy its predictability. It is the zany antics of the characters rather than the drama and uncertainty of the storylines which give the programme its appeal. But at the same time, the series has run for quite a few years and perhaps growing numbers of viewers are becoming tired of it. The only slightly black mark against the programme is the extent to which it features women. Although few viewers felt that women are treated badly, rather more felt that women could be featured more often.

Table 5.12 Perceived features of storyline and characterisation

	Agree %	Neither %	Disagree %
Survey 1			
Bad guys get just what they deserve	74	19	7
The good thing is that no one ever gets hurt	69	15	16
The storyline is the same sort of thing every week	68	15	17
It would be better if The A-Team did not always win so easily	42	24	34
The women who appear are treated badly	14	26	60
Survey 2			
The good guys and the bad guys are clearly distinguished	86	11	3
The storyline is usually very predictable	69	21	10
The programme is basically a bit of fun	68	18	14
The show does not feature women enough	37	36	27
The stories tend to differ a lot from week to week	34	30	36
The show has become very tired and repetitive	24	26	40

Table 5.13 Personal liking for The A-Team

	Agree %	Neither %	Disagree %
I hope that more series of The A-Team are shown on television in the future	54	24	22
If I watch it, it is usually because somebody else in the house wants to see it	38	12	50
I would like to see The A-Team still shown,			
in two years' time	30	29	51
in five years' time	19	24	57
in 10 years' time	13	18	69

Note: Survey 1 only

The A-Team is a much liked series (see Table 5.13). Despite its long run, more than half its viewers hope to see more series in the future, even if its desired "shelf life" may not extend as far as five years' time, and a similar proportion indicated that they watch because they want to see it and not just because somebody else in the house turns it on.

Children and Mr T

The character portrayed as the toughest member of *The A-Team* is played by Mr T. In addition to being incredibly strong, however, he is also shown as being particularly good with children. In the show, although Mr T intimidates and frightens the bad guys, children are depicted as feeling safe and comfortable with him. The attractiveness of Mr T (or the B.A. Baracus character he plays in the show) to children has led some commentators to suggest that he might serve as an undesirable role model. But what do children think about Mr T and which of his attributes stands out the most for young viewers? A recent survey has provided some interesting results.

In this nationwide survey, nearly 500 children indicated whether or not they wanted to be like each one in a list of 14 well known TV characters (Wober, Reardon and Fazal, 1987). Among a group of "male fantasy" characters was included Mr T. Of particular interest were the reasons children gave, in their own words, for wanting to be like Mr T when they grow up.

Asked to "write in your own words, or ask your mum or dad to write what you say about WHY you want to be like one of the people above..." 38 children wrote remarks only about Mr T; 16 others wrote about Mr T and about other characters as well. (Incidentally, 54 wrote about Anneka Rice, 41 about Tom and Jerry, and 30 about Cilla Black, while over a hundred wrote about mixtures of characters.)

Here are some of the remarks about Mr T, and one about Tom and Jerry.

> "Mr T helps people and is kind to children. He is not afraid of anything and is always smiling and makes sure people do the right thing."

> "Mr T is fun to be with and likes children. He does not get boring. I would like to be like B.A. because he is tough."

> "He can fight and he likes to help people and likes lots of children, I am 9 years old."

> "He is strong, and clever in his tactics, also his good humour although he seems to be nasty he helps other people in need a lot."

It seems clear that most children who admire Mr T do so because of attributes that he displays both outside as well as in the series. It is true, some did focus on aggressive aspects of Mr T:

"He's got a gun to shoot all the baddies."

"He has got weights and is very mad."

"Mr T has a bad personality so I definitely wouldn't be him."

"I like him when he has knocked the teeth down somebody's mouth."

But these four were the only aggression-loaded remarks about Mr T, compared with 34 of the more neutral kind. Identifications with *Tom and Jerry* seemed much more strategic, personal and humorous:

"I would like to be Jerry because I'd get chased about the room, and would have my own little hole to go to."

"I am like Tom – because I always catch my brother (who) pinches the food out of the fridge and I have to stop him."

It is useful to bear in mind , that while as many as half the children said they would like to be like a "male fantasy" character, this fell to less than a quarter of the 10-12 year olds. What has been found here is not unusual. A recent Dutch study found that Jerry (and then Tom) were the two most popular characters children found attractive – particularly among boys (Van der Voort, 1986). The Dutch researchers used the question: I'd really like to be like (whoever)" with three possible replies, from *true to not true*; they used a list of 45 characters altogether. Mr T was not included, but *The Incredible Hulk* was, and he was one amongst a "family" of characters who were good guys. A separate family of "bad guys" received low identification scores. It is clear that the Dutch children – like the British ones – "know" characters as good or as bad, and want to be like the good ones. Mr T is more widely seen as a good guy and children are quite capable of giving their reasons for this perception.

Concluding remarks

In this chapter, we continued our investigation of public opinions concerning the depiction of violence in selected TV crime drama series, focusing this time on US productions. Just as we found with British series, perceptions of violence in US crime dramas did not reveal widespread concern. Although there were differences in opinions given about different series, on the whole, a majority of our respondents who had watched episodes from these series did not perceive them to be excessively violent. This judgment was further reflected in opinions about the behaviour of fictional police and law enforcers in these programmes. Although many respondents did not feel that the use of violence by fictional police was nearly always justified, few felt that law-enforcers were overly violent either. These sorts of opinions were less positive or favourable with respect to a newcomer, *The Equalizer*, about which viewers' feelings were noticeably more mixed.

As with some British series, US productions were judged to be of questionable suitability for children who might, it was believed, take them seriously; but these programmes were seen as suitable for family viewing by a majority of respondents who watched them. This suggests, once again, that viewers believe it is all right for children to watch these series, provided they do so in the company of their parents. On the whole, however, all these series were widely appreciated.

Separate surveys were conducted to assess opinions towards *The A-Team* which revealed highly favourable opinions about the members of the team and the way they behaved. Most viewers did not perceive the show to be excessively violent – and few thought it was the most violent show on television. Violence was seen more often than not as being justified, but more importantly as unreal and acted out in a fantasy, humorous context. Few adult viewers felt that the show was unsuitable for or likely to disturb or frighten children, who it was believed, did not take the show seriously. Nor was *The A-Team* perceived to set bad examples for young viewers. Good guys are clearly distinguished from bad guys and the series was generally rated highly by most viewers.

If there were signs of a drop-off in popularity after a run of four years on British television, this may have had as much to do with the rather repetitive nature of the stories each week, as with the violence the show was perceived to contain. Finally, in a separate survey with children, evidence emerged that young viewers tended to perceive one member of *The A-Team*, namely Mr. T or B.A. Baracus, as basically a good person, and tended to focus their descriptions of him on his good, kindly qualities rather than on his tough, or aggressive behaviour.

CHAPTER SIX

OPINIONS ABOUT VIOLENCE IN NEWS AND CURRENT AFFAIRS

Real Violence and the Role of Television

The case is often made that grievous violence erupts from time to time and that an important function for television is to face society with the fissures in its structure. In Britain the conflict in Northern Ireland is one source of violence, usually occurring in the Province but also sometimes striking elsewhere. Other terrorist conflicts provide news of the victims of violence, while wars, ranging from long standing ones in the Gulf, Lebanon, Central America and elsewhere, to short ones such as the American attack on Libya, all add to the sources from which distressing scenes arise. Reported surveys indicate that the public considers television as its main source of news about world affairs, so there is a demand on the part of viewers for full and fair information about events, including conflicts. On the journalists' side there is a corresponding imperative to present reality, especially in its painful aspects in the belief that a well informed society, aware not only of the statistical facts but also of the pain of war will be in the best position to contribute through its political structures to promoting the case for peace.

The evidence now reported draws from surveys done over the past five years from the time of the Falklands war, and also relates to portrayals of the conflict in Northern Ireland, and riots in British cities. As with the world of fiction these results are not presented as a comprehensive account of viewers' opinions about the whole world of violence in reality and how it should be or is portrayed; nevertheless, they are gathered so as to provide as good an account as can be put together from IBA sources of public perceptions and questions on this topic.

First, though, it is worth examining results from a survey reported in 1978 in which respondents were presented with a list of news topics including four in which problems of military or civil violence played a prominent part (Wober, 1978). People were asked whether they felt that "for the general public, continuous coverage is needed", or "less should be shown"; then they answered "I myself would like to see ...... more than I do now"; or "less than I do now". For brevity the percentages who opt for the second alternative (less) are subtracted from the percentages opting for the first (more) and what the figures in Table 6.1 show is a net percentage; the operation was carried out in two ITV regions.

Table 6.1 Need to provide and interest in selected news topics

| | Net support for: | | | |
| | Coverage needed for public | | Own desire to see | |
Topics	Lancs %	Midlands %	Lancs %	Midlands %
Parliament	32	37	10	11
Royal Family	31	31	18	16
Problems of Northern Ireland	7	−2	−21	−26
Zimbabwe	−4	−4	−27	−21
Middle East conflict	−16	−7	−35	−18
National Front	−54	−52	−66	−53

SOURCE: IBA Research Report: *The Need for News*, 1978

A number of points emerge clearly from this table. First of all there is a close measure of agreement between the two samples, thus reinforcing the credence they both deserve. Next, there is a marked difference between the degree of feeling that topics should be carried – for the "general public", and individual willingness to see any such material. Finally, and of relevance to the present concerns, the four topics that would regularly contain portrayals of violence (Rhodesia at that time was still engaged in a war against rebel forces, while the National Front was creating some domestic stir through marches that led to civil disturbances) were obviously not what people themselves wanted to see. Only Northern Ireland among the four topics reached a "break even" point at which about as many people felt that continuous coverage was needed for public purposes, as who felt that the topic should recede somewhat from television news.

During 1981 there were two major series dealing with Ireland and the conflict in the North. In connection with these two programmes a survey was done in Ulster and an exactly parallel one in Yorkshire a fortnight later (Wober, 1981). Questions dealt with various aspects of violence in real life but also on perceptions of the two programme series and their role in reflecting the costs (and the origins) of a conflict for the viewing public. Table 6.2 deals first of all with some of the more general perceptions concerning violence – but it is to be borne in mind that the questions were asked in the context of the two programme series.

Table 6.2 Attitudes towards violence in society, with reference to Northern Ireland

Item – Agreement:	Score* from adults sampled in:	
	Yorkshire	Ulster
Parents should make a point of explaining to their children the causes of violence in the community	4.1	4.0
Violence is never an acceptable way to bring about social or political change	4.3	4.0
In real life Northern Ireland is not as violent as TV suggests	2.9	3.6
Economic conditions in this area are a more serious problem than violence	3.4	3.5
Too much attention is given to Northern Ireland in national TV news	3.3	3.3
Disagreement:		
I am afraid to walk alone in my own neighbourhood at night	2.5	2.3

* 5.00 = agree strongly, 1.00 = disagree strongly
SOURCE: IBA Research Report: *Broadcasting and the Conflict in Ireland, 1981*

In Ulster all the propositions were agreed with, except that respondents were afraid to walk alone at night. In particular, people agreed that life in Northern Ireland was "not as violent as TV suggests" – a proposition that was refuted by Yorkshire respondents, who however did not have the daily experience on which to test it out.

Both samples agreed that too much attention was given to Northern Ireland on TV news – supporting the results reported in Table 6.1. This leaves aside the question as to the role of special documentary series which can examine a question in greater depth. Opinions on this issue are now explored in Table 6.3. The figures are based on two sets of attributes describing reactions to the series; there were six positive attributes (informative, interesting, necessary to be shown, truthful, enjoyable and balanced) and three negative descriptions. The average result for the negative items was subtracted from that for the positive ones.

The result is a "net positive reaction" score, and it is this which the table examines. The top of the scale is 5 points (for agree strongly) and the bottom is 1 (for disagree strongly); thus 4 points cover the whole possible range of opinion and a "net positive reaction" of 1.0 means that people agreed with the positive statements considerably more than they agreed with negative statements.

Table 6.3 Net positive reactions to two series on Northern Ireland

| Sample: | | Net Positive Reaction Scores Concerning: | | | |
| | | Ireland–A TV history | | The Troubles | |
		Ulster	Yorkshire	Ulster	Yorkshire
Viewing experience of: Ireland:					
A TV History	Low	0.1	0.3	0.2	0.4
	Medium	0.6	0.8	0.6	0.3
	High	1.2	1.3	0.6	1.4
The Troubles	Low	0.2	0.4	0.1	0.4
	Medium	0.6	0.3	0.3	0.8
	High	0.6	1.4	0.8	1.1
Local News	Low	0.8	0.6	0.6	0.6
	Medium	0.2	0.9	0.4	1.2
	High	0.9	0.5	0.8	0.8

SOURCE: IBA Research Report: *Broadcasting and the Conflict in Ireland, 1981*

The final segment of this table provides a form of base line comparison by which to judge the patterns of opinions concerning the two particular series. Those who were heavy viewers of local news were not particularly likely to think more positively of the role of either of the Irish series than were light viewers of local news. This applied both in Ulster and in Yorkshire.

Turning to *Ireland – A TV History*, its heavy viewers were more likely to think positively of it than were its light viewers. This was true both in Ulster and in Yorkshire. There was something of a "cross over" effect in Yorkshire (though not in Ulster); in this, people who were heavy viewers of the *TV History* in Yorkshire also thought more positively about *The Troubles* (if they had seen any of the latter).

With regard to *The Troubles* (a shorter series, of five episodes compared with the *TV History* of 13 episodes), its heavy viewers were again more likely to think it had an overall positive function than were its light viewers. This applied less markedly in Ulster than in Yorkshire.

Again, there was a "cross-over effect" in which people who had seen more of *The Troubles* also thought more positively about the role of the *TV History*; again, this cross-over effect was noticeable in Yorkshire and not really in Ulster.

The overall outcome of this study was that the makers of these two series did so with high intentions, hoping to contribute to peace by furthering understanding – and those who were or who became interested enough to involve themselves in these series did think that a positive contribution had been made. There is certainly the opposite possibility, that the programmes might have been found partisan and increased irritation amongst viewers – which could eventually, at least in a few cases, be transformed into violent action; the research refutes this argument.

In 1982 Britain was involved in open hostilities against Argentina over the Falkland Islands. During the fighting there was very little action film shown on British television and a part of what was shown derived from Argentine sources. Although the military conditions were very much those of a war, British citizens in Argentina and Argentinians in Britain continued to live openly. This meant that British reporters were able to

Table 6.4 Attitudes to how TV might cover The Falklands Conflict

| Statements | % who believe TV should: | | | | |
	Show everything available on this from any source %	Show everything available - from UK or European TV %	Not sure %	Show only a part of what is available %	Show none of this kind of thing %
British citizens, if war is taking place, saying that we should not be in it	21	8	43	23	5
Argentine forces in action, dying or being wounded	18	3	25	37	6
British forces in action, dying or being wounded	14	5	32	42	7
British subjects, dying or wounded	14	4	39	38	5
Argentine bereaved families	11	4	37	40	8
British bereaved families	9	6	39	38	8

SOURCE: IBA Research Report: *The Falklands: Viewing Behaviour and Attitudes*, 1982

continue to file stories from Buenos Aires. It was possible therefore for television to show something of events in Argentina, as well as telling of the violence of the military confrontation and occasionally also showing it. Moreover, the victims of the fighting (wounded servicemen and bereaved families) were not infrequently televised. What did viewers think and feel about this war which could be seen from both sides? Table 6.4 offers some evidence, gathered at the outset before the invasion of the Falklands but after the retaking of South Georgia and while there were air raids and shelling (Wober, 1982).

Considerable written comments were gathered and these showed that several strands of opinion interconnected with each other: some people felt war in all its terrors should be shown, some distinguished between Argentine and British suffering (and responsibility), wanting to polarise the enemy from ourselves. The camp of candour was, however, smaller than that of restraint. In particular, people were reluctant to have innocent (as distinct from volunteer combatant) suffering shown, in the persons of bereaved families, but there was no effective distinction here between the possibilities of showing Argentine and British grief.

In summary, what is noteworthy here is the avoidance of a jingoist position and the presence of a more humane concern that exposure of privacy for the victims should not be added to the existing trauma and suffering they have to overcome of bereavement.

Summary of Attitudes Concerning the Portrayal of Violence in War and Conflict

It has not been the practice to ask viewers if they need to see death, destruction and suffering, to know if it is occurring; so research on viewers' attitudes to violence portrayed from wars and conflicts has generally approached the problem indirectly. When Britain was involved in the Falklands war research showed that clear majorities of people did not want television to show the carnage and indeed they thought that television should be restrained about showing the victims and the bereaved. While earlier responses had suggested that viewers showed no support for seeing "other people's" wars or even for it being shown without implying that they wished to see it, the Falklands revealed that viewers were also reluctant to be faced with the personal sufferings of "our own" war.

In the case of Northern Ireland, people tend to oppose its continued presence in the news; however, when two major and dedicated series went over the roots and nature of the conflict, not only were occasional viewers of these episodes to a net degree approving of the effort, but heavier viewers (though less so in Ulster itself) were much more approving of the positive role they felt was played by these series.

In all the surveys which touch upon the matter there is some call for greater depth of explanation. While pictures in television news may provide 'eyewitness' testimony of real life violence and conflict, it also has an important role to play in explaining why these events have occurred. A useful function of research in future may be to clarify in what ways viewers feel they are well served or not if the news telling goes further and attributes responsibility explicitly, or implicitly, for the sufferings unleashed in wars and conflicts.

Civil and Domestic Violence : Viewers' Attitudes

Apart from wars and military conflicts, civil disturbances provide another source of violent injury and death. These may be portrayed on television documentary and news, and this section explores public opinion in this area.

The 1980s have witnessed a number of major riots which have been

Table 6.5
"Experience" of riots by mediated means

Over the past few weeks there have been several
civil disturbances or riots in different places
in Britain such as Handsworth, Brixton, Toxteth
and Tottenham

		Class		
	All	ABC1	C2	DE
	%	%	%	%
Those who:saw a lot, on TV	57	57	58	57
read a lot, in newspapers	44	48	42	42
heard a lot, on the radio	27	32	24	21
Think that the *most detailed* coverage was				
on TV	53	46	60	57
in newspapers	17	23	14	11
on radio	3	3	3	3
all thoroughly realistic	12	13	10	13
not sure	14	14	13	16
Think that the *most realistic* coverage was				
on TV	55	47	63	59
in newspapers	8	12	6	6
on radio	4	4	3	3
all equally realistic	12	15	9	13
all equally unrealistic	3	3	3	3
don't know	18	19	17	16

SOURCE: IBA/BARB

vividly reported by television's news. Fire and fighting have become familiar sights; some have alleged that this familiarity has led sections of the disaffected population to be more ready to take part and the discussion of television's role has covered the issues of a duty to report the facts, to do so by showing the facts, the possibilities that portrayals produce imitation as well as limitation, under the theory that an informed and concerned public prompts its politicians to take remedial action. In 1986 questions were put to a national television opinion panel; first we can examine people's "experience" of riots through different message systems (see Table 6.5).

Television is clearly felt to be a copious source of news for a majority of people, with newspapers not far behind. But, while television was also emphatically cited as detailed and realistic, newspapers and radio were much further behind on these two characteristics. Very few people said that all three systems were equally *unrealistic*, but it is not possible to infer how many thought, or to what degree, that television (or newspapers or radio) was unrealistic or lacked detail. There is a small social class difference such that people of higher status are more likely to say they had detailed coverage in newspapers, than were people in the

Table 6.6 Opinions of TV's role in riots

	Agree %	Neither %	Disagree %
Whatever the social conditions are in these places, there is never any excuse for this kind of behaviour	83	9	8
Reporters should try harder to make sure that all sides have the chance to put their views across	80	13	7
It is very worrying to see on television the apparent inability of the police to control these situations	68	16	16
Coverage of disturbances like these only encourages other people to copy what they see happening	61	19	20
Television coverage has made many people much more sympathetic towards the police	50	29	21
It is not surprising that these incidents happen given the social problems that exist in some parts of the country	44	22	34
Television coverage has made many people realise that there are often good reasons for these incidents	26	28	46

SOURCE: IBA/BARB

lowest social grouping. It can be said, therefore, that for the unemployed television was the most vivid source of information about the riots (it was also so amongst the comfortably well-off, but not by such a large margin over newspapers). Did viewers think there was any likelihood of imitation? (see Table 6.6).

Six out of ten respondents believed that television coverage of riots could incite others to imitation. There was much more support, however, for the idea that television coverage may have stimulated support for the police, than the reverse – either that it has not stimulated support for the police, or that it may have engendered understanding of rioters' actions. These themes are further illustrated in Table 6.7.

Table 6.7 Viewers' beliefs about reasons for riots

Which of the following, if any, would you say are the main reason for these disturbances?	Those who say the item is main reason for riots			
	All	**12-34**	**35-54**	**55+**
Inadequate Restraints				
Lack of self-control among the young	77	71	75	86
Too little parental control	74	65	76	85
Over-soft policing in these areas	31	27	27	39
External Stimuli: "Avoidable Provocations"				
Political agitation from outside the areas concerned	64	55	67	74
Too much media attention to these riots	43	37	44	50
External Stimuli: Other				
Social conditions like unemployment, or housing	50	58	50	38
Over-harsh policing of these areas	21	25	21	17

SOURCE: IBA/BARB

The theme of inadequate restraint is the most widely supported notion – and in all three aspects explored, it was older people who were more convinced of this reason for the disturbances.

The idea of provocation divides into two subsets – one which is more prominent in the thinking of older people, and where there is an implication that interference, if there, is mischievous or just ill-advised; the other aspect of provocation is more "structural" since social conditions like unemployment or poor housing are the product of deep-rooted processes which are difficult to improve at a local level. With this is the perception of over-harsh policing that can be interpreted as a defence of the poor social conditions. Here, older people are less emphatic advocates than are younger ones. This does not stem from the possibility that older people are better-off materially – they may be as likely to be unemployed and poor themselves; the difference here may have to do with hope – less evident among the young, less necessary among the old. However, whether by imitation or irritation (the difference between vivid portrayals on the screen of the good life available in Britain, and the reality in some sections of cities) there is a substantial – even if not favourite – view that "media attention" has been excessive and not beneficial.

Concluding remarks

The reality of violence as a part of everyday life is brought into our homes in nightly news broadcasts which carry stories of conflicts and disturbances from around the world. And occasionally, pictures from the site of violent confrontation can make us eyewitnesses to such events. In this chapter we have reported several surveys which investigated public opinion regarding the coverage in news and current affairs programmes on television of wars, terrorism and civil disturbances. Topics covered included Northern Ireland, the Falklands conflict, and inner city riots in Britain.

In one survey respondents both in England and Northern Ireland were more likely to agree than to disagree that too much attention was given on the news to Northern Ireland. Other opinions revealed, however, that two television documentary series about the troubles in the province were felt to have made a positive contribution.

At the time of the Falklands conflict strict controls were laid down and implemented over the flow of information from the islands. The viewers had mixed opinions about how much should be shown. Many, however, were undecided or favoured some restraint in reporting. Around four out of ten wanted to see something of the British and Argentine forces in action, including pictures of the dying and injured. The majority opinion was that considerable care should be taken over the showing of innocent suffering, such as that experienced by bereaved families.

Surveys which dealt with news coverage of civil disturbances or riots in inner city areas such as Handsworth, Brixton and Toxteth revealed that television was identified as the most important and most realistic source of information. Opinions about the nature of the coverage revealed mixed feelings, however. Television news was perceived to have enhanced understanding in some respects, but not in others. Most respondents felt that the news had clearly shown the problems faced by the police in having to control these violent disturbances. But many also felt that it did not always provide adequate explanation as to why these incidents occurred in the first place. Many respondents also indicated some concern that television coverage of riots could encourage imitation.

CHAPTER SEVEN

PUBLIC OPINION AND STATUTORY REGULATION AND CONTROL OF TELEVISION VIOLENCE

It is possible to describe two "models" of control with regard to the output and the use of television. Each of these models is a clarified or simplified view of where responsibilities should lie and of who should take what action to ensure that good and not harm should come of the experience of communication by broadcast. In practice neither of these models forms an unmodified blueprint for the actual state of affairs either in Britain, or in most other countries; but it is useful to describe the two models in order to get a better understanding of a mass of often conflicting claims, opinions, emotions and ideas. In clarifying the two opposite ways of handling responsibilities we will find valid positions for all the opinions described in this monograph.

One model of responsibility sets the onus for decision on the individual. This way of doing things can be seen to have roots in the philosophy of Thomas Paine and the actions of Jefferson and Benjamin Franklin in America. These were men who preached and practised the merits of self-reliance and independence based on a highly inquisitive and informed citizenry, served by small publishers of print. Carried into the present, this way of going about affairs finds those who expect viewers to prevent any harms upon themselves or their families from screen fare of whatever character, by regulating their own viewing using the off-switch and powers of selection and critical analysis. This model regards it as extremely important for the opinions of viewers to be expressed. These opinions can inform programme makers and broadcasters, as well as other viewers, who may then make their subsequent judgements on what to watch (and how) with the aid of a fully informed account of public opinion which is, however, critically analysed by each observer just as programmes are.

The other model of responsibility sets the onus for decisions on delegated experts. Such an approach implies that however well informed or intentioned, the ordinary person cannot make the best decisions about such things as foods that should not be eaten, drugs that should not be used, and in the world of screen fare, programmes or their possible contents that should not be seen singly or in combination. In the realm of television it is this model in which calls are made for greater control at the point of origination, of programme content and scheduling. It is this approach indeed, which provides the *raison d'etre* for the Broadcasting Act which assigns a wide and complex role to the IBA.

It is important to realise that much of the British discussion of programme effects (more often concerned with harms than benefit) springs from and implies a need to operate within this second, delegated model of responsibility control. It may be ironic that most of the experimental and developmental literature on the harmful effects of screen violence comes from America, where there is not only a large measure of violent material available, but also the closest approximation to the autonomous-responsibility model in operation that it is possible to find in any country. Yet in spite of their numerous studies reporting harmful effects of violent portrayals (as well as some which do not substantiate harmful effects) the very scientists involved all refrain from advocating centralised restraints and join most other public voices in that society in calling for more effective self-control on the part of individuals. In Britain on the other hand, as we indicate in Chapter 1, much of the anxiety about the (much less prevalent) phenomenon of violence is linked with implications or quite open urging that stronger centralised controls should be exercised.

In practice, Britain's television system is not an example of either of the "pure" models of responsibility, but combines aspects of both. To a considerable extent there is delegated responsibility and centralised control; but to a considerable extent there is both scope and need for individual responsibility and self-control. It would be interesting to have public opinion evidence on the matter where the responsibilities lay mostly with the centralised control authorities. Indeed, it is evident that in Soviet bloc countries centralised control is strong and public opinion polling is scarce to the point of non-existence; similarly the American communications researcher Douglas Boyd has stated that in some Arab countries research on public opinion about broadcast fare is ruled out as not just unnecessary but also undesirable. Conversely, it is necessary to have open and copious reflection of public opinion in a society where responsibilities are carried individually. With the British situation somewhere in between, there is both a need for and an interest in attending to public opinion on the matter of screened fare, including violence; but at the same time it must be clearly understood that it is not purely public opinion which propels and shapes broadcasters' actions.

In practice, this "hybrid" situation can give rise to at least four possible neat combinations of public opinion and broadcasters' action. In one combination, broadcasters show what people say they want to see – this is harmonious, and probably is what happens most of the time. Examples include the genres of light entertainment, sport and soap opera. In another combination, broadcasters do not show what the majority of the public assert should not be shown – examples being extremes of violent and erotic behaviour combined with violent fiction. A third position is when people do want to have material shown and broadcasters withhold it – and of this it is less easy, if at all possible to find examples; and finally there is material which broadcasters want to show but which few of the public want to see. Examples here might include avant garde material as well as the more highly demanding categories of information programming.

What we are concerned with in this report is more like what can arise in the third combination above, as well as with examples possibly on the borderlines of the fourth – both of these being patterns when the opinions of the public may differ somewhat from the implied "opinions" expressed in the practice of the broadcasters. There is also the variant of the first situation, where broadcasters provide what people say they want to see, but where specialist opinions hold out from the generality and argue that both the public and the broadcasters are wrong. Here we get the judgement that the segment (and it may well be a majority segment) of the public that wants and gets some commodity has exercised this demand misguidedly. Some harm will come from the transaction of which people are not fully aware, or which they refute if they are asked about it.

A final and indispensable item of context that it is necessary to draw into the scene of the present report is the Broadcasting Act (of 1981) whose statutes cover the Independent Television and Radio systems, which contains at least three portions which, taken together, make this work necessary. In one section (4-(1)-(a)) it is stated that as far as possible nothing should be broadcast which "offends against good taste or decency...". This injunction is concerned with a subjective psychological reaction. The "litmus" for this reaction is necessarily a measure of public opinion. This has to be preceded by the application of expert discretion which observes, and sometimes negotiates and modifies, what goes forward to be broadcast. Ultimately, however, the test of whether offence has (or vastly more often has not) occurred lies in asking viewers about this. This is done in various ways, by noting spontaneous response, by attending to advisory committees and, as in the report here, by systematically representative surveys of public opinion.

This last point corresponds with another portion of the Act (45-(1)) in which it is explicitly stated that the IBA shall be informed about the state of public opinion concerning the programmes broadcast (and programmes are held by a subsequent paragraph (3) to apply as well to advertisements). The third ruling of the Act which is clearly relevant to the phenomenon of the portrayal of violence is one in which the broadcasters are required not to show material which may be conducive to public disorder; in a phrase which follows immediately after the one cited, above, concerning offence against good taste, the sentence goes on to say "or is likely to encourage or incite to crime or to lead to disorder ...". Now while these injunctions may be understood to refer to group phenomena such as riots, they can also reasonably be seen to apply to individual acts of aggression or destructiveness, even those which may be reflectively turned against the self. Here is where the connection is made with the broadcasters' concern not to prompt ideas of suicide attempts.

In the past two years the press has carried a great deal of comment on and criticism of the television services. Bearing in mind our two models of responsibility, much of this commentary drives towards implementing a "tighter" version of delegated care. It is true that other analyses and criticisms can be found, advocating less central control; but, where these opinions deal with responsibilities and effects they tend to be fewer and more sophisticated rather than populist in tone. Quite a separate field of discussion arises from the world of technical development and here the pressure for more supply of screened material (whether reaching the user by cable, satellite, combined or other means is not relevant to the present analysis) does not often acknowledge but certainly implies a movement towards an individual model of responsibility. For the time being, however, the social and political questions of with whom responsibility lies and of what kind are not often elaborated within discourses on technological developments; so what remains is, indeed, quite a strong pressure upon the broadcasting authorities to tighten their work of control and thereby to increase the extent to which they take responsibility on behalf of the individual viewer and of society.

A few of the critics include in their case the notion that the public broadly agree that there is too much screened violence, that it should be reduced, and that viewers are offended by much of what there is. This touches upon the public opinion data which are available, and, starting with the question of offence, it is possible to demonstrate that this is not a widespread phenomenon. The actual proportion of the public who say they were offended at some time during the past year by some violence on the screen lies between ten and twenty percent.

Beyond the variations of sampling error, the figures of offence taken from violence portrayals are best seen in terms of three comparisons. One is across time, and it appears that over a period of a dozen years the proportions reporting this kind of offence tended to fall for the first six and then to have somewhat irregularly risen again before showing a slight decline once again most recently. The second comparison is with other sources of offence, coded as bad language and sex. Language has always been more commonly cited than has violence though it is not clear why or what the relevance of this fact may be. One reason why it happens may relate to the meaning which people attach to the word "offence". Colloquially, this applies better to infringements of manners and propriety within the world of otherwise harmonious social relations. Acts of violence immediately take one beyond this world and may not be related to, judged or described in terms of, offensiveness. Therefore it is not the most appropriate measure of public opinion about scenes of violence to use the concept of offence as the instrument or scale. It may be something like using the thermometer alone, to measure discomfort; it has come to be realised that humidity is another indicator of comfort possibly more important than temperature. The latter is certainly part of the picture and its usefulness is increased if its limitations are also understood. The same case is true with the measure of offensiveness with which to assess public reactions to screened violence. This is useful, but does not give the whole picture.

Public opinion can be measured in other ways. One method is to provide statements which provide explicit expressions of opinion with which respondents may either agree or disagree. In many of the surveys we have reported in this monograph, this was the method used. Statements of opinion were general notions about violence on television and aspects or ingredients of normal television series. Although the nature of the items and the style in which they were presented were similar in both instances, the important distinction between these two kinds of survey is that in the latter case, respondents were asked questions about particular programmes they had watched and therefore, more so than in the former case, had a specific point of reference with respect to which they could frame their opinions.

In the most general of terms, respondents who agreed with the sentiments that there is too much violence on television or that it causes social harms outnumbered those who disagreed. When asked to give these same kinds of opinions about particular programmes they had watched, however, the patterns of responses were quite different. Far fewer tended to perceive excessive amounts of violence for personal tastes or to believe that specific television series caused real harm.

One particular part of the population which is believed to be especially vulnerable is children. In our surveys, respondents tended to agree that it would be better to delay experience of screen violence until children are older; and here we enter another of the realms of paradox that crop up from time to time where contradictions exist between opinions and actions. Our respondents indicated that parents should be more careful about these matters, and that too few parents are skilful in this regard. It

67

was difficult, however, to find any substantial proportions who said that their own exercise of responsibility with regard to their children has been faulty. Nevertheless, a variety of experiences is acknowledged and, for respondents who had watched episodes of action adventure series with their own children aged between six and ten, as few as five percent said the experience of viewing *The A-Team* or *Magnum* may have been harmful, while as many as 40 percent of those who reported having watched *Hill Street Blues* or *Miami Vice* considered this experience may have been harmful for their children.

Those who call for tighter central controls imply a distrust in the ability of the broader public to know and to take responsibility effectively for itself; the case is that watching lethal violence acted out on screen, portrayed essentially as painless and the outcome of amusing exploits of the forces of good, accomplishes two kinds of harm. One is that such portrayals may encourage similar behaviour among viewers (imitation); the other is that the viewers' sensitivities to such behaviour become blunted (desensitisation).

In neither case has conclusive evidence emerged to substantiate their occurrence contingent upon watching the sort of material normally seen on the major broadcast television channels in this country. Furthermore, there is some British evidence with a children's panel that these mechanisms may not, in the first place, receive much opportunity to take place. One major reason for this is because the overall amount of such material viewed is actually not large and because that particular viewing experience is diversified in any case (or diluted) by a wide variety of other and less contentious materials (Greenberg, Gunter, Wober and Fazal, 1986).

What does the public think, then, should be done with regard to control? The two-model spectrum of responsibility was put before a large sample of viewers and they rejected each extreme form by large majorities. The majority did not want a situation (involving lethal violence, or bad language) where such things are simply never shown; they also equally rejected a situation of maximum openness in which such things are shown and it is simply left to the viewer to leave it or to take it (and digest it healthily) according to one's own responsibility. There was clear support for a situation that rests between these alternatives, where there are protections offered by a variety of measures such as information and warnings, and scheduling at particular times and places.

The public's "prospective" opinion, looking forward as it were to what should be done about controls is complemented here by a range of reactions that are retrospective and which evaluate the performance of the broadcasting authorities in the ways in which they have provided material containing violence. The attitude items referred to here included four which were positive in evaluation and four negative ones; viewers were first of all divided into three groups, by their own testimony comprising heavy (four hours or more a day), light (two hours a day or less) and intermediate viewers. What was being tested was not just the position of the public as a whole in evaluating the climate or environment of screened violence but also a proposition put forward by the American researcher Professor George Gerbner. This holds that heavy viewers become acclimatised in their opinions, coming to accept the mores and ethical standards of what they see on television, while light viewers may be more critically independent.

What was found here certainly does not contradict this theory and may support it. In more detail, light viewers approved the positive statements more strongly than they agreed with the negative ones. To this extent the broadcasters have a verdict of approval from amongst the potentially more critical segment of the public. The heavier the viewers, however, the more they supported the positive (as well as the negative) statements; but the increase in support for negative statements was only slight, while that for the positive ones was much more marked. In total therefore the heavier viewers give a much more positive verdict about the actual climate of control than do lighter viewers (who are on balance positive in any case).

At least three things need to be said about this result. One is that heavier viewers are much more likely to see a wider range of television's contents and thus have more relevant experience on which to base their judgements than have light viewers. This consideration, taken alone, would underline the favourable nature of the overall result, for an assessment of broadcasters' practices. However, introducing another paradox, if Gerbner is right then the process of acclimatisation would mean not only that heavier viewers are more lenient or full of praise, but that they are now more *parti pris* and in this sense less objective and more subjective judges of what they are evaluating. It is very difficult to deal with this alternative interpretation, but this brings us to the third necessary observation. This is that heavy viewers are not just that, but they tend also to be older and of lower social status than lighter viewers, and these attributes are also linked with differences of attitude and of judgement. In short, it may not be weight of viewing experience but psychological differences linked with demographic status that have produced the effects described. To help us clear up this difficulty it would have been necessary to have performed some slightly more complicated statistical analysis than the system allowed at the time the information was collected. This would be quite useful to carry out, and it may be done at some further date.

The sum of all that has been found about opinion on violence in the realm of drama and entertainment is that people are not widely offended by it – it is not likely that they should be, as offence is not the appropriate criterion of concern; looking back on what they have seen, even light viewers deliver a positive 'net' verdict on the amount and positioning and use of violence in screen fare, but heavy viewers are even more positive in their net judgement. These perceptions of what is currently achieved in British broadcast practice are given about a phenomenon about which the public say there is every reason to have care and concern. They indicate that they believe that screen violence can be of harm and that it needs to be controlled. The public do not want to be 'left alone' to their own devices with an unregulated supply of violence (or of sex or of bad language) but they certainly do not want such potentially problematic material swept off the screen altogether. Large numbers of people say they watch entertainment programmes containing violence, even with young children, and the majority say they are harmless entertainment – though this does leave small proportions of the population, albeit probably amounting to some tens of thousands per episode, who say the experience of viewing may have been harmful for their children.

It is probably fair to say that all this portrays the British viewing public as very moderate in its outlook, requirements and experience with regard to drama and entertainment and the ways in which this may include violence; and it portrays the public as having been served in a like manner by broadcasting in which, overall, the amount and disposition of violence has been moderate and well managed. This says nothing about the realm of real life violence which news and current affairs programming are bound to deal with in one way or another.

Surveys on the treatment of violent conflicts ranging from long running to short wars and from military to civilian strife have shown a widely recognised and easily understandable phenomenon in this field. This is that people consider that such material should be shown, but are much less inclined to want to see it themselves. In keeping with much of what was reported in the realm of fiction, only small proportions called for full portrayals of the reality and suffering of battle; the largest proportions of people wanted the broadcasters to use editorial restraint over what they would show. The world of reality involves questions of bias or of political evenhandedness in portraying violence; here, it is noticeable how ready British viewers were to have an opponent's opinions and position portrayed, as witnessed in the case of Argentina and of the IRA in Northern Ireland where the opponents are seen in "old-fashioned" terms as an enemy.

In most of these cases public opinion was in favour of greater depth of explanation but also for some restraint. Thus there is a sizeable segment of concern that televising of civil strife may act as an example or catalyst for further actions of this kind. Nevertheless, when television tackles the roots and problems of conflict and strife, viewers tend to react in more favourable terms.

In short, both within the realms of fiction and of fact, notwithstanding a number of difficulties which this monograph has done its best to detect and to understand, the public's opinion can be seen to be one which is accustomed to and which approves a system of regulation which shares responsibility between the broadcaster and the viewer in a manner which has evolved over a long period of practice.

References

Greenberg, B., Gunter, B., Wober, M., and Fazal, S. (1986) *Children and Their Media*, London: Independent Broadcasting Authority, Research Report.

Gunter, B. (1985) *Dimensions of Television Violence*, Aldershot, England: Gower.

Van der Voort, T.H.A. (1986) *Television Violence: A child's eye view*. Amsterdam: Elsevier Science Publishing Company.

Wober, M. (1978) *The Need for News*, London: Independent Broadcasting Authority, Research Report.

Wober, M. (1981) *Broadcasting and the Conflict in Ireland*. London: Independent Broadcasting Authority, Research Report.

Wober, M. (1982) *The Falklands: Viewing Behaviour and Attitudes*, London: Independent Broadcasting Authority, Research Report.

Wober, M., Reardon, G., and Fazal, S. (1987) *Personality, character aspirations and patterns of viewing among children*. London: Independent Broadcasting Authority, Research Report.

Technical Appendix

The research discussed in this monograph derives from four sources:

1.
The IBA's annual Attitudes to Broadcasting survey which has been conducted every year since 1970 (except for 1978). This survey normally consists of face-to-face interviews with a quota sample of around 1,000 adults (aged 16 years and over) living in the United Kingdom. Sampling points are selected so as to be geographically representative of all mainland areas of the country. Quotas are set by age, social class and employment status within sex for each region.

2.
The IBA's regional Audience Reaction Assessment survey which ran for approximately ten years until 1984. This served not only to provide data on audience appreciation of programme output on television, but also facilitated the investigation of viewers' opinions about programmes in more detail. Each week Television Diaries were sent to a sample of viewers. The objective was to achieve opinions from at least 500 people aged 16 years and over, who were representative of viewers in the area surveyed in terms of age, sex and social class. On alternate weeks the sample was drawn from a panel in Greater London, and in intervening weeks from other Independent Television areas in Britain.

3.
The IBA's Children's View survey which measured young viewers' appreciation of programmes. This survey ran for around 10 years until 1986. In addition, opinions about programmes were probed in more detail. The survey took place six times a year among a national sample of around 700-800 children aged 4 – 12 years, who were representative in terms of age, sex and social class of children generally.

4.
Questions placed by the IBA on a national Television Opinion Panel (TOP) which is supervised by the Broadcasters' Audience Research Board (BARB). This panel consists of a weekly achieved sample of 3,000 respondents aged 12 years and over. The TOP is administered by post. Each week the panel member receives a booklet to cover 7 days' programmes running from Monday through to Sunday. The booklet is designed to canvass viewers' appreciation for each programme seen, more detailed reactions about particular aspects of programmes and detailed opinions about more general topics related to television viewing. The panel is designed to be nationally representative and is selected with controls for total weight of viewing, channel preference, social class and marginal controls for sex, age, presence of children in household and size of household.